English Furniture

Mirror and Side table (painted). *c.*1735
From Wentworth Woodhouse, Yorkshire

ENGLISH FURNITURE

John C. Rogers ARIBA

Revised and enlarged by Margaret Jourdain

Spring Books

First published 1923 by Country Life Ltd
Third, revised, edition published 1929 by Country Life Ltd
Revised edition © Copyright Mrs B. I. Rogers and
Basil Marsden-Smedley as Executor of the late
Miss Margaret Jourdain, 1959

This edition published 1967 by Spring Books,
Hamlyn House · The Centre · Feltham · Middlesex

Printed in Great Britain by Fletcher & Son Ltd, Norwich
and bound by Richard Clay (The Chaucer Press) Ltd, Bungay, Suffolk

CONTENTS

WORKING DIAGRAMS IN THE TEXT

ILLUSTRATIONS

ILLUSTRATIONS

THE PERIOD OF MAHOGANY FURNITURE

PREFACE

THE author of *English Furniture*, the late John C. Rogers, was a practising architect, who was responsible for the conservative and sympathetic restoration of a number of ancient buildings, including extensive repairs to the roof of St. Alban's Abbey. From his youth he had devoted himself to the study of English domestic furniture and woodwork, and had acquired a wide knowledge of the methods and construction employed by carpenters, joiners and cabinet-makers throughout the long evolution of English furniture.

English Furniture was published in 1923 after Macquoid's *History of English Furniture*. In *English Furniture*, John Rogers approached furniture from a different angle; the historical background was briefly summarized, but his interest lay in construction; and the precise and workmanlike analyses of types of furniture were accompanied by diagrams which are of value to the student and the ever-widening circle of those interested in the art of the English craftsman. Research during the last quarter of a century has made it necessary to re-arrange, revise and amplify the introductory and historical chapters, but there is little to add to the technical sections, which have not been, nor are likely to be, superseded. Examples of mediaeval furniture are so rare that they have been excluded from the present edition, and fuller treatment is given to furniture of the late Georgian period.

1949   MARGARET JOURDAIN

PREFACE TO REVISED EDITION, 1959

IN preparing this revised edition, the opportunity has been taken to add photographs of certain articles of furniture that, although the subject of sections in the text, were not illustrated in the previous edition. These include a cradle dated 1641, a corner cupboard *c.* 1715, and a washstand *c.* 1770.

PART ONE

THE PERIOD OF OAK FURNITURE

From the reign of Elizabeth to circa 1685

I

HISTORICAL NOTE

ENGLISH furniture from the middle ages to the Restoration of monarchy was almost entirely of oak, and according to William Harrison,[1] writing late in Queen Elizabeth's reign, 'nothing but oak was any whit regarded'. English oak is a timber which has been described as 'the most beautiful oak in the world, . . . preferred above all others for its fine quality, rich colour and endurance'.[2]

In miniatures in illustrated manuscripts, furniture including settles, stools, chests, reading desks, and framed cupboards for the display of plate, is represented as coloured, and from this evidence, and from the coloured decoration of church screens, and the traces of colour found in some pieces of domestic furniture it may be concluded that mediaeval furniture was painted.

The surface of the wood was generally lime-whitened, followed by a polychrome scheme of decoration carried out in oil colour or in tempera. About the middle of the sixteenth century the surface of the oak was sometimes left in its natural state; in other cases, at time of manufacture, poppy or linseed oil, often dyed with alkanet root, was rubbed in. In the seventeenth century beeswax with turpentine was used in polishing and renovating the surfaces, the primary object being to preserve the wood.

With the exception of chests, furniture of Gothic character is of extreme rarity, some few cupboards of plank construction, and side tables fitted with a cupboard being almost the sole survivors.

During the last quarter of the sixteenth century a large bulbous excrescence, borrowed from the Low Countries, appears on table legs and on supports of cupboards. This member is divided by a moulding into a clearly marked cup and cover. During the late seventeenth century this *motif* loses its significance.

A characteristic of Elizabethan carving is an all-over richness and undisciplined elaboration in which strapwork, demifigures, masks and grotesques are combined together to fill a given field without the 'consecutive motive and preciseness' of French and Flemish art of the same period. There is a lack of finish in

[1] *Historical description of the Island of Britaine* (prefixed to Holinshed's *Chronicles* 1587).
[2] Quoted in Elmes and Henry, *Trees of Great Britain and Ireland*, p. 338.

English carving in which tool marks are plainly visible. During the first part of the seventeenth century strapwork runs riot as an enrichment. Towards the close of Queen Elizabeth's reign, upholstered seat furniture is mentioned and examples of seat furniture covered in rich materials and provided with cushions dating from James I's reign is preserved at Knole.

During the reign of James I, the raised ornament is usually flat and unmodelled and rarely projects beyond the face of the wood, the effect being that of an unmodelled fret. To throw up this slight ornament, the ground is often matted. In the succeeding reign, there is less abuse of strapwork and there appears in some examples an architectural bias. Features such as pilasters, pediments and capitals are frequently used decoratively.

During the second half of the seventeenth century the enrichment of case furniture by split turnings in the form of balusters, pendants and bosses, was introduced from the Low Countries. These turnings were stained black and glued to the surface of the piece. The years of Civil warfare and the eleven years of the Commonwealth were characterised by a check in production. In seat furniture, seats and backs were sometimes stuffed and covered with plain or decorated leather. In general, furniture shows a simplified variation of Jacobean forms.

II

WOODWORK AND CONSTRUCTION

ENGLISH oak is the most durable of all growths, but it is also the most tricky to work, and the importance attached to the seasoning processes was a vital element in ensuring that work would remain sound. The trees being of ripe age, and having been felled and barked at the right seasons, the logs were immersed in a running stream, after which, having been allowed to dry out, they were taken to the sawpits and converted into planks, boards, and beams.

It appears that little oak was converted by saw prior to the latter part of the sixteenth century, the mediaeval method having been the employment of the beetle and wedge, by which scantlings were split from the log. The roofs of many buildings retain their original rafters of split oak. In finishing split oak for furniture the surfaces were trimmed with the adze, the marks of which are discernible on many pieces, especially on the backs of panels.

The two-handed saw worked almost vertically, was operated by two men, one above and the other below the log (called top and bottom sawyer); and the pair kept together, as it was essential to know each other's stroke and throw.

A long period ensued during which the planks lay in the open, above ground, and were kept apart to allow the complete circulation of air; in this way the oak became dry and mellow. However long the process, when a new surface was exposed by saw or plane, the effect of the atmosphere would cause it to move, and for this reason there was no attempt to hurry the work. In fact, it was the tradition to pass from one job to another in the workshop, allowing the work to take up its final 'set' before tightening up the tenons and securing with the oak dowel pegs. In this period glue was little used.

In the sawyer's work of conversion, two methods have always been employed. One utilizes almost every square inch of the log; and the other is wasteful of a certain amount; but judging by the oak furniture remaining, it was more often adopted. By the first method the tree was sawn down in parallel planks, which gradually diminish in width on each side from the central plank. The result of this treatment is that, with the exception of a few central boards, the edges reveal the silver grain where it can have no value, the broad surfaces showing very plain and uninteresting grain. By the second method figured oak is provided on every board. The tree is first quartered in the direction of its length, then each triangular quarter is sawn into planks by cuts that follow the radiating lines known as medullary rays, which are the silver grain or figure. The boards so produced would not be so wide as those obtained by the first method, but its general use results in boards of superior hardness, durability, and freedom from a tendency to warp. The silver grain, being practically free from cellular structure, reduces shrinkage to a minimum.

The earliest method of construction in articles such as chests and cupboards consisted in pinning planks together by oak pins or nails. This method of nailing by iron nails remained in use for rough boxes and chests as late as the early eighteenth century. The planks for large chests were necessarily thicker than those used in the construction of small chests and boxes.

The introduction of panelled framing from the Low Countries in the fifteenth century solved the problem of constructing areas which did not suffer warping, splitting and shrinkage. The panels, cut to the required size, were trimmed on every side, to fit into grooves in the rectangular framework of rails and styles. The joints connecting the rails and styles are united by mortise and tenon, secured by square cut oak pegs driven through circular holes. The fact that the heads of these pegs or pins often project slightly beyond the surface of the frame is due to the shrinkage of the wood of the latter.

The term 'joint' applied in inventories to furniture (which is a variant of *joined*) was used to distinguish it from furniture which was turned, and in which the parts were not united by mortise and tenon. The specification and valuation in inventories indicate the higher value of *joined* furniture.

Oak was the prevailing timber for English furniture during this period, and though walnut pieces are listed in English inventories, these were in many cases foreign-made.

When the mediaeval practice of painting furniture declined in the sixteenth century, it was customary to preserve wood by rubbing it with oil. In addition, beeswax was used, which did not darken the surface, but formed a protective film upon it. Instances are recorded of varnishing furniture during the late sixteenth century.

Inlay in reserves cut out of a solid ground, mainly in two-coloured woods (holly and bog oak) was employed in oak and walnut furniture of the second half of the sixteenth and seventeenth centuries. The outlines of the pattern were first marked on the ground to be decorated, sinking these surfaces about one eighth of an inch within these lines, and fitting therein small pieces of contrasting woods. Besides holly and bog oak, ash, beech, fruit wood, yew, sycamore and poplar were employed.

CONVERSION of TIMBER INTO PLANKS E^{TC}

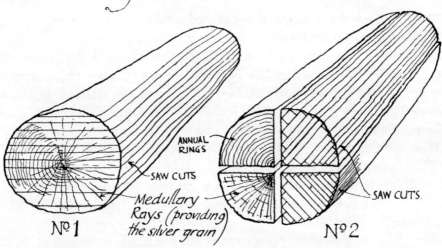

N°1. Tree trunk shewing most economical cutting, which in oak does not reveal the silver grain (except at the diameter)

N°2 Tree trunk "quartered" or rift sawn, shewing method of cutting oak to obtain figured surfaces.

III

CHESTS

THE chest was the principal piece of mediaeval furniture, serving for storage, and on occasion as a travelling trunk and also as a seat.

The terms coffer, ark, standard and hutch were in use for varieties of chest. The coffer, defined in the *New English Dictionary* as 'a box chest, especially a strong box in which money and valuables were kept', was often of small size and its wooden carcase was covered with leather or other material. It was defined by Randle Holme in 1688 having a 'circular' lid or cover, as distinct from the chest, which has a flat lid. Standards were large chests used for carrying goods.

The hutch (derived from the French *huche*) is applied to a receptacle of box form with one or more doors in front, for example Sudbury's[1] Hutch in Louth Church, in which the doors are carved with profile portraits of Henry VII and his wife, Elizabeth of York.[2]

The majority of Gothic chests were of massive plank construction. In that at Stoke D'Abernon Church, which dates from the thirteenth century, front and back are formed of three planks, the central one placed horizontally and butting upon the other two, which are arranged vertically and are carried lower to form feet; the ends are cross-braced over a solid board. This type appears to have continued until well into the fifteenth century, though there were many variations in which the construction was masked by architectural features, such as buttresses and applied tracery; and the width of the stiles greatly decreased. Towards the close of the fifteenth century a simple chest was evolved in which the sides were carried lower than front and back to form feet, the members being united by iron straps and, or by iron nails or oak dowel pegs.

The top was attached with wrought-iron strap hinges secured with nails; but in some cases, in place of hinges, iron wire staples linked together formed a hinge. In the sixteenth and seventeenth centuries, this type of chest became modified. Reduced in size and made of six thin boards (five-eighths to three quarters of an inch) it continued in use for many years after panelled construction was adopted.

[1] *Academy of Armory* (1688) Book III, chapter XIV.
[2] *Dictionary of English Furniture*, vol. II, s.v. Hutch.

CHEST CONSTRUCTION

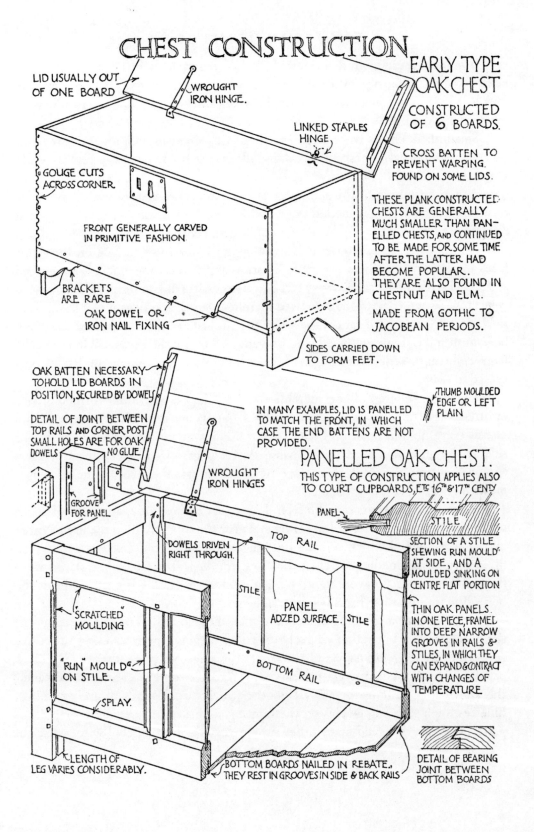

EARLY TYPE OAK CHEST

CONSTRUCTED OF 6 BOARDS.

LID USUALLY OUT OF ONE BOARD

WROUGHT IRON HINGE.

LINKED STAPLES HINGE

CROSS BATTEN TO PREVENT WARPING. FOUND ON SOME LIDS.

GOUGE CUTS ACROSS CORNER.

THESE PLANK CONSTRUCTED CHESTS ARE GENERALLY MUCH SMALLER THAN PAN-ELLED CHESTS, AND CONTINUED TO BE MADE FOR SOME TIME AFTER THE LATTER HAD BECOME POPULAR. THEY ARE ALSO FOUND IN CHESTNUT AND ELM.

FRONT GENERALLY CARVED IN PRIMITIVE FASHION.

MADE FROM GOTHIC TO JACOBEAN PERIODS.

BRACKETS ARE RARE.

OAK DOWEL OR IRON NAIL FIXING

SIDES CARRIED DOWN TO FORM FEET.

OAK BATTEN NECESSARY TO HOLD LID BOARDS IN POSITION, SECURED BY DOWELS

THUMB MOULDED EDGE OR LEFT PLAIN

IN MANY EXAMPLES, LID IS PANELLED TO MATCH THE FRONT, IN WHICH CASE THE END BATTENS ARE NOT PROVIDED.

DETAIL OF JOINT BETWEEN TOP RAILS AND CORNER POST SMALL HOLES ARE FOR OAK DOWELS NO GLUE.

GROOVE FOR PANEL

WROUGHT IRON HINGES

PANELLED OAK CHEST.

THIS TYPE OF CONSTRUCTION APPLIES ALSO TO COURT CUPBOARDS, ETC 16TH & 17TH CENTY

PANEL

STILE

DOWELS DRIVEN RIGHT THROUGH.

TOP RAIL

SECTION OF A STILE SHEWING RUN MOULD AT SIDE., AND A MOULDED SINKING ON CENTRE FLAT PORTION

"SCRATCHED" MOULDING

STILE

PANEL ADZED SURFACE.

STILE

THIN OAK PANELS. IN ONE PIECE, FRAMED INTO DEEP NARROW GROOVES IN RAILS & STILES, IN WHICH THEY CAN EXPAND & CONTRACT WITH CHANGES OF TEMPERATURE

"RUN" MOULDG ON STILE.

SPLAY.

BOTTOM RAIL

LENGTH OF LEG VARIES CONSIDERABLY.

BOTTOM BOARDS NAILED IN REBATE. THEY REST IN GROOVES IN SIDE & BACK RAILS

DETAIL OF BEARING JOINT BETWEEN BOTTOM BOARDS

Iron locks let in from the external face were invariably fitted, a hinged staple being fixed on the inside of the lid, which, when the latter was shut, entered the lock by a hole in the face-plate; the staple, when free, also serving as a handle with which to lift the lid.

Small plank chests were often enriched with slight mouldings and low relief carving. Besides oak, chestnut wood and elm were used, but very few of these woods have survived.

At the beginning of the sixteenth century the panel system was adopted for furniture construction. Panelled chests which are rare prior to Elizabeth's reign became general in the last quarter of the sixteenth century.

An important characteristic of oak framing is the flush surface on the outer faces of all joints, such as junctions of stiles with rails, and under-framing and stretchers with the legs; this was a structural necessity, due to the pegs being placed very close to the edge of the mortised member. When the pegs were driven into the holes, it would have caused the wood to split had not the shoulder of the tenon been flush and tight up to the edge to prevent it. This method was still in use in the later eighteenth-century mahogany work, long after the reason for its use had ceased to exist.

Chests were often of considerable size, and the lid was either formed of two or three boards or was panelled to match the front. When of the former type, the lid boards were held in position by a cross-bearer placed transversely on the under side at the ends and fixed with several dowel pegs; when shut, these bearers appeared outside the chest. Another type of bearer was fixed across the end edges of the lid boards, also pegged on.

A small box with its own lid from four to six inches wide, and the full depth of the chest, was often framed in at one end near the top, entailing the use of three extra pieces, one of which was the lid, hinging on small round projections which fitted into corresponding holes in the chest framing. The side and bottom were housed in grooves, so avoiding all nailing, and necessitating the fitting in of the box while the chest itself was being assembled.

Enrichment varied between simple mouldings on the framing surrounding the panels to rich but rather coarsely executed carving, often covering the entire surfaces of framing and panels of the front, the sides being less ornate. The back panels, though moulded, were not carved. A favourite type was the arcaded panel, the arch being built up or carved on the panel, also a series of arches, flutes, lunettes, or interlacing circles on the framing. Types of arabesque or strap-work patterns, gouge cuts, and many other simple devices of direct tool work trick out the surface. A reserve was sometimes left in the centre of a band of ornament, in which were carved initials or name, and a date. A class of chests termed 'Nonsuch chests' from a fancied resemblance to Henry VIII's palace at Cheam, is distinctive in character, and is decorated with marquetry representing stylized buildings, at a time when inlay was used.

The mouldings surrounding the panels are important. On many examples they consist of two types, the first being the 'scratched' mould, which is not continuous, but dies out on the surface, to leave a plain, square edge where the uprights butt against the rails. It is to be found in most cases along the bottom edge of the top rail, and also on the inner edges of the corner posts.

The second is a moulding of more comely profile, run continuously on both edges of the intermediate uprights, or styles; it is cut off square to butt against the top rail, and at the bottom the moulded stile is cut back on the splay to accord with the splayed top edge of the bottom rail, a curious feature which always obtained, and suggest the 'weathering' of a cill. This splay (also termed a chamfer), is on some chests found stopped with a moulded finish in Gothic manner on either side of the junction with each style, instead of the ordinary continuous splay. In all cases these mouldings are part of the member on which they appear.

Chests of Elizabethan character continued to be made throughout the seventeenth century in country districts, but changes in decoration and construction appeared during James I's reign. The sides and backs were panelled, joinery was improved, and the construction less solid. The crude, scratched mould was often replaced by the continuous 'run' variety (in most cases still part of the solid framing) and the mitring at the corners is an advance in skill. The splay on the top edge of the bottom rail was still often used, and an important moulding planted on around the base just above the feet. Floral and pattern carving are met with, but the variety of the carvers' work gave way to a use of stock ornament, which consisted of repeats carved on long strips and cut off to suit the dimensions of the piece under construction without regard to the spacing of the pattern. The more characteristic chests were enriched with split turnings glued on, chiefly on styles and rails. The arch which appears in the panel, closely resembles its contemporary in masonry. Low relief strap work was also general, and is often found on the boxes which were made in great numbers at this period and through the Commonwealth, their construction being similar to the small type of plank chests. The lids of the large chests were generally panelled, and the edge had a thumb mould. These types of chest decoration continued into Charles I's reign; but mouldings, as a general rule, were much shallower. Much play was made of mitring the mouldings

23

in and out around the panels, and this necessitated their being run on separate strips of oak, to be very accurately fitted and glued and bradded in position. Chests of this type were made for the remainder of the seventeenth century and well into the eighteenth. During the seventeenth century a small metal escutcheon placed over the keyhole took the place of the lockplate.

The 'mule chest' is a transition between the chest and the chest of drawers. These chests first appeared about 1590, and were made with one or two drawers placed beneath the box portion; the drawers had stout sides, which were grooved to slide on the early form of runner, and rough dovetailing was attempted; the bottom boards were placed transversely and fixed with nails.

Illustrations on pages 41 to 43.

IV

CHAIRS

THE scarcity of chairs is due to their rarity in use until the early seventeenth century. Chairs were provided with arms, and the single chair did not come into general use until the mid-seventeenth century. In domestic use the chair was the seat of the master and mistress of the house. At Hengrave in 1603 the dining chamber was furnished with two great chairs, one little scrowled chayre and nine stools.[1] There were three types of chairs used in the early years of the Renaissance, a cross-framed (or folding chair), an enclosed chair with panelled back and arms, and a turned (or thrown) chair of simple construction.

Cross-framed or folding chairs, which appear in miniatures and illustrated manuscripts, depended upon their garnishing with textiles, and were limited to the Royal palaces and great houses. The seat supported a cushion resting on webbing. In an oak chair in the sacristy of York Minster[2] the back was originally hung with a panel of velvet, strained on leather from the top to the spring of the arms.

In a variant on the cross-framed chair the cushioned seat was no longer loose. Among the rare examples of chairs dating from James I's reign at Knole, the cross-framed lower portion is covered with textile in some instances.

In a well-preserved chair[3] of similar type in the Victoria and Albert Museum, the frame-work of soft wood is entirely covered with velvet, trimmed at the edges of the seat and arms with a fringed galon. The back and cross-frame is bordered with a galon fixed with close-set brass nails.

Turned (or thrown) chairs which were made by the turner, and not by the joiner, were constructed of posts and rails, in which the units fit into sockets. These chairs, 'a rustic survival of the traditional mediaeval[4] chair seen in illustrated

[1] Gage, *History of Hengrave*, pp. 26-27.

[2] *Age of Oak* (fig. 47). Traces of the panel were still visible in 1836 and are shown in Shaw's *Ancient Furniture*.

[3] W. 12-1928.

[4] Victoria and Albert Museum *Catalogue of English Furniture and Woodwork*, Vol. 1 (Gothic and early Tudor), 1923, pp. 3-4.

manuscripts' continued to be made until the close of the seventeenth century, in the marches of Wales, Lancashire and Cheshire. In the simple form the chair often consisted of a triangular seat, stout posts and back rail, with smaller turned spars or turnings connecting the seat frame with the stretcher and the central post with the back rail. In its later form, dating from the late seventeenth century, a number of ornamental bobbins, pendants and free rings were added to the structure. Turned chairs exist in a great variety of woods, elm, ash, beech, fruit wood, mulberry and yew, and it is evident that the turner used whatever wood was available in the district where he worked.

Joined chairs are defined in the *Academy of Armory*[1] (1688) as 'all made of joyners work'. In some early specimens the space beneath the seat was enclosed with panelling, and the front panel or the seat was hinged, forming a cupboard. In the succeeding type the front legs were baluster turned, and continued above the seat as a support for the arms, the latter being of rectangular section, shaped, with rounded ends. Flat, rectangular rear legs were continued up as back supports.

The back was framed up with one or two panels, the top rail (in the sixteenth-century chairs) was usually fixed between the uprights and tenoned into them; but early in the seventeenth century it was placed either to ride across the uprights as a cresting (the latter being tenoned up into it) or the cresting began to extend on either side, and ears or brackets were added to the sides of the uprights. These latter features, however, are known on late Elizabethan armchairs, but under the Stuarts became more exaggerated. The carving shows decline in character and skill of execution. Rectangular stretchers, in some cases moulded, united the legs, and the seat board was thin and quite flat, often with a slight mould on its projecting edge.

About the time of the Commonwealth, single chairs were made in sets. The construction of the seat and leg framing was similar to the armchairs, but there was a tendency to fix the front stretcher higher up the legs; and on some chairs there were two rows of stretchers. Many examples of panel back chairs which are dated, show this form persisting throughout most of the seventeenth century. A form of armchair with a narrow back known in France as the *cacqueteuse* (a conversation chair) was adopted in Scotland.

In the type known as Yorkshire and Derbyshire chairs (of which examples date from the Commonwealth and late seventeenth century) the back is filled in with arcading between the top and bottom rail, or by two rails of arched or horse-shoe form. About 1650 the seat boards, instead of oversailing the rails, were in some

[1] Book III, chapter XIV, p. 14.

26

examples framed in, so providing a shallow sinking for a flat cushion or squab. At this date there was also ornamentation of split, turned bobbins to the faces of the back uprights. Chairs became lighter in construction, and as the century advanced more use was made of turning. During the Commonwealth a chair with a horizontal panel at shoulder height, and seat covered in leather, turkey work, or needlework, secured at the edges with large brass-headed nails was introduced.

Until about 1660 the turning which was generally in simple baluster forms, was more scholarly in proportions and detail than the earlier designs. But about this date the early hand-cut twist or spiral was attempted in oak, though it is rare before the Restoration, when it was improved by the lathe-turned twist. Towards the end of the Commonwealth the number of stretchers appear to have decreased; on many chairs there was one at each side, another placed transversely and connecting them at their centres, also one in front and possibly one at the back, placed half-way up the legs. Frequently all were turned, plain squares being left on legs and stretchers, where they were mortised and tenoned one to another; on these squares all arrises and corners were rounded off. This type of chair continued in use throughout Charles II's reign. The 'table chair', a combination piece of furniture which served a dual purpose, appears as early as 1547 and continued to be made throughout the seventeenth century. In this, the underside of the table-top is fitted with two rails, which are hinged to the arms by pins, thus allowing the back to rest upon the arms. The top is also secured when horizontal by wooden pins which are inserted through the arm-rests and rails.

Illustrations on pages 44-47, 49 and 52.

V

STOOLS AND FORMS

THE importance of the stool lay in its being the only kind of portable seat, for Evelyn writing of the generation before his own, states that 'nothing was moveable save joynt stools'.[1] Stools and forms (the latter being of massive trestle type, or an elongated stool) were frequently made in sets to go with the table, and were of such a size that when not in use they were placed under the table and piled on the stretchers. The construction and design of turning and carving on stools followed the character of the table to which they belonged. They are framed up with deep rails under the board seat and stretcher rails a few inches off the ground but the legs straddle outwards. Viewed front or back, they are parallel and vertical; also, in some cases the seat inclines slightly towards the front, that is, the side placed nearest the table.

Illustrations on page 48.

[1] *Miscellaneous Writings* (ed. 1825) p. 700.

VI

CUPBOARDS

REFERENCES to 'livery' cupboards often occur in inventories, but their character has not been defined.

A few small and primitive cupboards are in existence which belong to the borderland of the late fifteenth and sixteenth century. In these the wide planks forming the structure are finished near the edge with a channel moulding, and the interior is shelved.

The method of piercing the panels with tracery was utilized to ventilate the interior, the piercings taking the form of Gothic tracery. A later type was the hanging cupboard, in which the front was largely composed of turned balusters, or spindles. In these the doors were generally hung on wrought-iron hinges, and were secured with a lock, or by a turn-buckle (a small wooden bar pivoted near its centre, so that when turned, it engages the edge of the door).

A few hanging 'dole' cupboards are found in churches, where they served (and still serve) to contain bread distributed to the poor. There are two examples at St. Alban's Abbey, dating from the early years of Charles I's reign, which are still used for bread given by the bequest of Robert Skelton in 1628. There are also open dole-shelves serving the same purpose.

From the second part of the sixteenth century, two main types of furniture for the service of meals were evolved, an enclosed cupboard, and a table or open stand on which cups and plate were placed. The latter form has recently been recognized as the court cupboard[1] which make a frequent appearance in sixteenth century inventories and is described as having carpets or covers for its tiers.

These court cupboards were in general use during the second half of the sixteenth century and until the Restoration. They consisted, in their simplest form, of three large shelves for the display of plate and dishes, being supported at the two back corners by flat posts, and at the front corners by two tiers of carved bulbous columns. Some specimens of the late sixteenth and seventeenth centuries had the space between the top and middle shelves enclosed with panels and doors,

[1] O. Baker, *In Shakespeare's Warwickshire*, p. 254.

the front being flat. The columns gave place to baluster turned supports of smaller diameter. The shelves which were moulded on edge and held down by oak dowels were only about half an inch thick.

Under the two upper shelves a frieze was usually formed, in the lower of which (*i.e.* the middle shelf) it was general to form a drawer on grooved runners. In some examples the cupboard between the top and middle shelves had canted sides, always panelled and generally carved. Soon after the Restoration, these court cupboards went out of fashion. Large two-storied enclosed cupboards, of which many examples exist, were formerly called court cupboards though the French term *court* (short) was inapplicable. These were in general use in large establishments for more than a century after 1550. The lower part was fitted with shelves and faced with doors, over which came a thin top, and above this rose a short and shallow cupboard topped with a cornice. At the two front corners a bulbous column was usually placed, which in the sixteenth-century examples, was frequently carved with acanthus leaf and capped with quasi-Ionic volutes. About 1620 the column supports were turned in squat baluster and vase forms. In Charles I's reign the columns tend to disappear entirely, and as a reminder of their former use turned knobs depend from the cornice.

The top cupboard had splayed sides in some cases, allowing more room for display. Both the upper and lower stages are enclosed by doors. The upper stage is usually divided into three sections, but in some instances the central section is fixed. The large lower doors appear to have had iron hinges in all cases, but the small upper doors frequently swung on oak dowels, fixed vertically between top and bottom rails of the door and framing, while the whole piece was being assembled.

The wrought-iron hinges on late sixteenth-century and the seventeenth-century examples were kept small, though still showing on the face. They interfered very little with the moulded and carved stiles and posts, and their most usual form was a wedge or butterfly shape, being narrowest on the knuckle. They were always secured with iron nails. Other types of hinge used were the ornamental 'cockhead' and the H. This method of hinging the doors was altered on many of the cabinet chests of the Commonwealth and Charles II periods, in which the doors extend to the full width of the piece, so that the hinges show only when the doors are opened, and are very similar in shape to our modern 'butt' hinge. In country districts, particularly in the north, the cupboard was made until the opening of the eighteenth century, and on similar lines to examples one hundred years earlier.

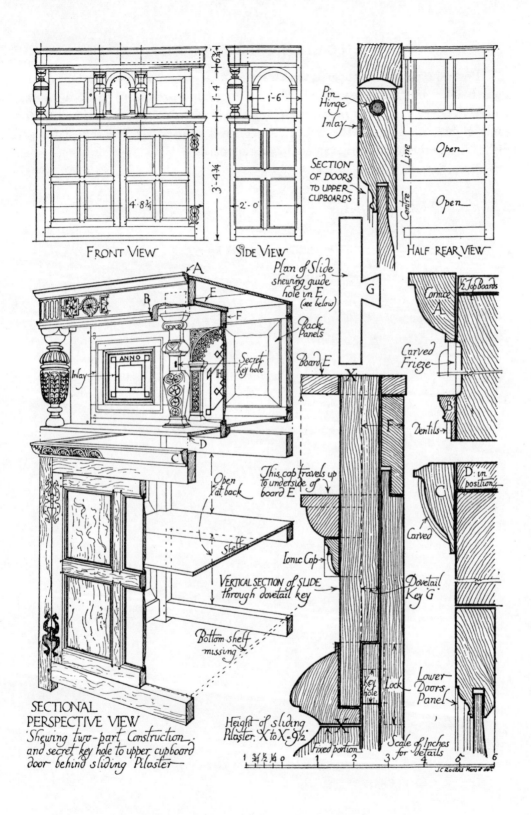

FRONT VIEW

6¾·

1·4·

3·4¾·

4·8¾·

SIDE VIEW

1·6·

2·0·

Pin
Hinge
Inlay

SECTION
OF DOORS
TO UPPER
CUPBOARDS

HALF REAR VIEW

Centre Line

Open

Open

A

B

E

F

Inlay

ANNO

Secret
Key hole

H

D

C

Open
at back

Shelf

VERTICAL SECTION of SLIDE
through dovetail key

Bottom shelf
missing

Plan of Slide
shewing guide
hole in E
(see below)

Back
Panels

Board E

G

X

F

This cap travels up
to underside of
board E

Ionic Cap

Cornice
A

½ Top Boards

Carved
Frieze

Dentils

B

D: in
position

C

Carved

Dovetail
Key G

Lower
Doors
Panel

SECTIONAL
PERSPECTIVE VIEW
Shewing two-part Construction
and secret key hole to upper cupboard
door behind sliding Pilaster

Height of sliding
Pilaster, X to X = 9½·

Fixed portion

Key
hole

Lock

Scale of Inches
for details

1 ¾½¼ 0   1   2   3   4   5   6

J.C. Rogers Mans del.

Post-Restoration cupboards which are of great size, and of greater length than their height, are frequently dated. Three-tiered cupboards were made in Wales, where they are known as *tridarns*. During the latter part of the seventeenth and early eighteenth century the upper tier forms a dresser for keeping plates and dishes, while the lower forms an enclosed cupboard.

Illustrations on pages 53-57.

VII

TABLES

THE earliest type of table was of trestle construction. The trestle supports were either independent or were held in position by one or two stretcher beams; the latter were tusk-tenoned through the trestles, being 'pulled up' tight by oak wedges passing through holes in the tusks. In this way they could be dismantled and reassembled with ease. The top was made up of three or four massive planks with cross-battens on the under side, which registered its position on the top of the trestles. The board and the trestles were separately listed in inventories. The joined table, with its top fixed to the under framing appeared to be sixteenth century.

About the middle of the sixteenth century the draw table (a device imported from Flanders) came into use, and being capable of extension to almost double length by pulling out a pair of under leaves superseded the earlier type. The diagrams (p. 35) explain the mechanism of this device. Turned legs were placed at the four corners, which in the Elizabethan examples were richly carved. The under frame was tenoned into the tops of the legs (which were left square above the enrichment), and connecting stretcher rails were provided just above ground level. The under-framing provided a frieze for decoration, which on fine examples was carved or inlaid on all sides.

Stretchers had two phases, the earlier type having a flat member fixed along the top surface and projecting on each side, so making it T-shaped in section. But about the commencement of the seventeenth century this appears to have given place to the normal rectangular section, often slightly moulded.

Long dining tables with a single fixed top were often made for great establishments, having six or eight legs, but the width seldom exceeded three feet. In side tables on four or six legs, similar in design, the frieze was only carved on the front. Table tops were formed of massive planks with cross-framed ends, and (when not designed as draw tables) were held in position by under battens, or by a number of oak dowels driven down into the under-framing.

The first quarter of the seventeenth century saw little change in these heavy oak tables. The draw table, however, appears to have gone out of fashion by the accession of Charles I. About 1625 another, smaller, type of oak table was in general use. Its construction was light, and when designed as a side table it had one or two drawers in the frieze. These drawers were arranged directly under the top, there being no locking rail in the frieze or under-framing, and prior to 1660 the sides were grooved for runners. The legs were turned in baluster, ball, reel, and knob forms, left square where the stretchers tenoned into them. The legs were also turned into a type of vase-shaped foot. The tops, which measured about three feet in width by two feet in depth, were always thin, and with thumb moulded edges, and were dowelled down to the framing. The later pieces show the influence of walnut designs, such as twist-turned legs, and flat-shaped stretchers (which in some were placed diagonally).

Small tables with a falling leaf or leaves supported on a swinging leg, appear early in the seventeenth century, and were set against the wall as side tables when the top was not extended. Gate-leg tables which mark a departure in design, were made in large numbers.

There are about twelve different types known. The legs varied in number from four to twelve, and the shapes of the top, when extended, were square, oblong, octagonal, circular, and elliptical. The type generally found has eight legs in two rows of four, with varied baluster turning. The stretchers on many were left square, of the same scantling as the legs, and two top edges were relieved by a slight bead mould. On richer examples the stretchers were turned, though not always to match the legs; for instance, the legs of a table may be turned with a vase surmounted by the spiral twist, and the stretchers will have turning in baluster forms adjusted to suit their lengths. Of the four legs on either side, two compose the gate, each gate being framed up with top and bottom stretchers, with one of the legs pivoted to the main framing. The gates swing out to support flaps hinged to the centre board on the under side with a pair of small wrought-iron hinges, which were secured with nails until the introduction of screws in the second half of the seventeenth century.

All framing joints are the mortice and tenon with oak dowel pegs; but in the mahogany gate-leg tables the joints were not pegged, as glue was then used, and framing was cramped while it set. If design and size permitted, a drawer was usually fitted; and on some large tables two were provided. They were set in the under-framing, and had a special carriage and runner in the form of a horizontal slat of oak fixed longitudinally in the drawer space, and upon which the centre of the drawer bottom could slide; side bottom runners are known, but are rare. The top was composed of three pieces, the centre section being secured with oak or

OAK DRAW~TABLE

ELIZABETHAN & EARLY JACOBEAN
circa 1575~1625

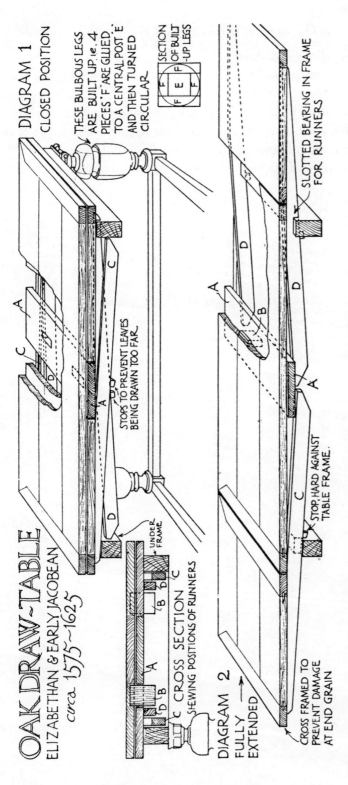

DIAGRAM 1
CLOSED POSITION

THESE BULBOUS LEGS ARE BUILT UP. i.e. 4 PIECES 'F' ARE GLUED TO A CENTRAL POST E AND THEN TURNED CIRCULAR.

SECTION OF BUILT UP LEGS

STOPS TO PREVENT LEAVES BEING DRAWN TOO FAR.

SLOTTED BEARING IN FRAME FOR RUNNERS

UNDER FRAME

CROSS SECTION SHEWING POSITIONS OF RUNNERS

DIAGRAM 2
FULLY EXTENDED ⟶

STOP, HARD AGAINST TABLE FRAME.

CROSS FRAMED TO PREVENT DAMAGE AT END GRAIN

THESE TABLES ARE CONSTRUCTED WITH STOUT UNDER-FRAME AND STRETCHERS UNITING THE FOUR LEGS USUALLY, THE PLANK 'A' IS PLACED TRANSVERSELY CENTRAL AND FIXED DOWN TO THE UNDER-FRAME: THIS MEMBER HAS TWO RECTANGULAR SLOTS CUT THROUGH IT WHICH ACT AS GUIDES TO TWO HORNS 'B'. THESE HORNS-ORTUSKS,- ARE HOUSED INTO, AND PROJECT BENEATH THE UNDER SURFACE OF THE MAIN TABLE TOP, TO WHICH THEY ACT AS RIDING ANCHORS WHEN THAT MEMBER GRADUALLY RISES AND FALLS DURING THE OPERATION OF DRAWING OUT THE TWO UNDER LEAVES.
WHEN THE TABLE IS CLOSED, EACH UNDER-LEAF IS IN LINE WITH THE CENTRAL PLANK 'A'. BOTH LEAVES HAVE TWO LONG ARM RUNNERS FIXED ON THEIR UNDERSIDES, MARKED C-C & D-D. THE AFTER-ENDS OF WHICH ARE FREE, AND SLOPE AT THE CORRECT ANGLE TO PERMIT OF THE LEAVES ARRIVING AT THE LEVEL OF THE CENTRAL TABLE TOP WHEN DRAWN OUT. THE LEVERAGE ON THE EXTENDED LEAVES BEING COUNTER-ACTED BY THE RUNNER ENDS BEARING ON PLANK 'A'.

walnut dowels, according to the wood used, but in the case of eighteenth-century examples, screws were generally used to secure it from underneath on the inside of the framing. The joints between these top sections were either square, groove and tongue, or rule joint, all of which were in use in the seventeenth century, but the last named superseded the others in the eighteenth century. The edges of the top were finished with a thumb mould in certain cases, but it was usually a 'softened' square edge. A page of diagrams is given explaining the features of these tables (page 179).

Illustrations on pages 58-61.

VIII

BEDS

O F BEDS of the early Tudor period, little has survived but slender carved
posts (and in rare cases, the head board). Examples of carved bedposts in
the Victoria and Albert Museum which are carved with geometrical
ornament, measure from two and three quarters inches in thickness to four inches.
A set of four posts[1] have grooves into which the head board was fitted, and on the
capitals are iron hooks and rings for the textile covering.

The earliest instance of a four post bed with a framed back (colour) and
tester is the bed[2] from Crackenthorpe Hall, Westmorland, which represents 'the
intermediate link, hitherto missing, between the fragments of Gothic bedsteads
(sets of posts and head board) in the Victoria and Albert Museum, and the fully
developed type.[3]

In the four post bed in the Saffron Walden Museum, dating from the early
years of the sixteenth century, there is no tester, the head board is panelled and
the posts are carved with small enriched geometrical compartments above a fluted
base. There is a fragment of a bed in the Victoria and Albert Museum, which
probably formed part of an example without a tester; in this the head board is
panelled and on either side is a short baluster-shaped post, one of which has its
original finial[4], an eagle. There are a number of extant examples dating from the
late sixteenth and early seventeenth centuries, ornate structures with panelled and
carved head framing supporting the returns of a carved and moulded cornice, and
a tester frame, The front corners of the tester were supported by columns swelling
out into one or more bulbous forms, often topped with crude Ionic caps, the
shafts were fluted, gadrooned, or enriched with arabesques and strap work. These
columns were carried on pedestals with moulded caps and bases, panelled on all
sides and often carved.

1 Victoria and Albert Museum, W. 18, 1911.
2 Victoria and Albert Museum, W. 12, 1943.
3 Ralph Edwards, *Country Life*, July 5, 1946. The bed dates between 1525-1540.
4 Victoria and Albert Museum, W. 834, 1898.

The bed frame itself was low, and was attached to the head framing only; at the foot it stood free on its own legs. The side rails were holed and grooved for the cord lacing by which the stout canvas or rush-matting mattress was held taut, and this held the tenons of the side rails securely in their mortices in the corner posts.

A form of bed devoid of tester and columns was like some wooden beds of to-day, except that head and foot were connected by oak side beams. The head, about four feet high, was panelled, the foot was very low (in some cases enriched with a row of short turned balusters between rails). The corner posts were stout and usually turned.

Illustration on page 62.

IX

CRADLES

CRADLES take the form of a low rectangular box, generally rising at one end in a hood. There are posts at the rocking corners, finished at top with a turned finial, and the four sides are panelled. Under the ends cross-bearers are fixed, shaped as rockers. On those more carefully finished an inscription, initials and date are often found.

Illustration on page 43.

X

CHESTS OF DRAWERS

THE chest of drawers, which has been defined as 'a kind of large box or frame with a set of drawers, formerly used for keeping money and other valuables, now an article of bedroom furniture', was known in the sixteenth century but makes a rare appearance in inventories until the second half of the seventeenth century. The terms used for drawers were 'tills', and 'drawing boxes'. During the latter half of the sixteenth century, a drawer was first fitted at the base of the chest.

The chest of drawers appears to have been made in fairly large numbers, soon after the Restoration. Mouldings were planted on the carcase framing and on the drawer fronts to give panel effects in rectangular designs, entailing mitres of various angles and accurate fitting. A favourite treatment was to form two distinct panels on the face of one drawer, giving the effect of two drawers, though the deception is never complete on account of the central keyhole. During the second quarter of the seventeenth century a type of sub-cornice divided the chest a little above half its height, and below this projection a pair of panelled doors were hung to enclose three or four drawers. About 1660 the doors were omitted, and all drawers were exposed.

On the side panelling, the frieze, and the drawer fronts, split turned bobbins and egg shapes frequently stained black to simulate ebony were often applied. The corner posts or styles of the frame were carried down as supports, but frequently the latter were bun-shaped or bracket feet; and occasionally a separate stand was added, consisting of shallow arches with five or six short turned legs. Several oak chests of drawers which are inlaid with picturesque decoration in bone, ivory and mother-of-pearl, and bear dates ranging from 1650 to 1665, appear to be entirely of English creation.

Illustrations on page 63.

1. CHEST, formed of planks pegged together, the sides prolonged to form feet. The centre carved with the arms of Noel, and the date 1620, flanked by panels carved with the gouge and V-tool. From Mr. G. C. Stirling.

Height, 2 ft 1 in   *Length*, 3 ft 8 ins

2. CHEST, the front carved with three arches, the angles with terminal figures. Early years of the seventeenth century. From Mr. S. W. Wolsey.

Height, 2 ft 3 ins   *Length*, 4 ft 6 ins

3. BACK OF A DESK, inlaid with stylised buildings in coloured woods (Nonsuch inlay). Late sixteenth century. From the Victoria and Albert Museum.

Height, 1 ft
Length, 2 ft 3 ins

4. DESK, inlaid with arabesques in holly, box and sycamore, stained green and brown. Late sixteenth century. Col. N. R. Colville.

Height, 9½ ins
Length, 1 ft 4½ ins

5. CHEST, the front carved with linen fold. Early sixteenth century. From the Harold Peto Collection.

Height, 2 ft
Length, 4 ft

6. CHEST, carved and inlaid, the base fitted with two drawers. *c.* 1620. From the G. L. Riley Collection.

Height, 2 ft 8½ ins   *Length*, 4 ft 5 ins

7. CRADLE, with scrolled cresting and turned finials; the upper panels carved with the date 1641 and the owner's initials. From the Victoria and Albert Museum.

Height, 2 ft   *Length*, 3 ft   *Depth*, 1 ft 4 ins

8. CHAIR, with lunette-shaped cresting (Lancashire type). Mid-seventeenth century. From Chetham's Hospital, Manchester.

Height, 1 ft 9 ins   *Width,* 1 ft 7 ins

9. ARMCHAIR, turned; late seventeenth century. From Browsholme Hall, Yorkshire.

Height, 3 ft 11½ ins   *Width,* 2 ft 4½ ins

10. ARMCHAIR, the back surmounted by a lunette, the back panel inlaid in dark and light woods. *c.* 1600. From the James Thursby-Pelham Collection.

Height, 4 ft 2¼ ins   *Width,* 2 ft 1 in

11. CHAIR, the frame decorated with bobbin turning. *c.* 1660–1670. From the James Montagu Collection, Cold Overton Hall, Leicestershire.

    Height, 3 ft ¼ in   *Width,* 1 ft 6¾ ins

12. CHAIR, the tall back carved with scroll-work, and dated in the cresting 1641. The front of the seat rail is inlaid with holly and box, and the front legs and stretcher bobbin-turned. 1641. From the Victoria and Albert Museum.

    Height, 3 ft 10 ins   *Width,* 1 ft 9 ins

13. CHAIR, with crescent-shaped top and cross rail, the front legs and stretcher turned. (Yorkshire and Derbyshire type.) Mid-seventeenth century. From the Victoria and Albert Museum.

    Height, 3 ft 4¾ ins   *Width,* 1 ft 6¼ ins

14. ARMCHAIR, the back panel incised with the date 1625, and initials.

15. CHAIR, with knob-turned front legs and seat and back panel covered with leather. Commonwealth period. From the James Montagu Collection, Cold Overton Hall, Leicestershire.

Height, 3 ft 1½ ins *Width*, 1 ft 8½ ins

16. ARMCHAIR, the back divided into panels carved with a floral spray and scroll work, surmounted by a pierced and carved cresting. The legs and arm supports of columnar form. *c.* 1620. From Brigadier W. Clark.

Height, 4 ft 2 ins *Width*, 2 ft 2 ins

17. CHAIR, the seat and back covered with velvet (on which needlework *motifs* are applied). Early years of seventeenth century. From the Duke of Devonshire, Hardwick Hall, Derbyshire.

Height, 3 ft 3 ins

18. CHAIR, with spiral turning on front legs and stretcher, the back and seat covered with turkey work and fringed. *c.* 1660–1670. From Holyrood House, Edinburgh.

19. BENCH, early seventeenth century. From Sizergh Castle, Westmorland.
Height, 1 ft 10 ins   *Length*, 7 ft 6¾ ins

20. STOOLS, with feet of columnar form. Early seventeenth century. From Mr. S. W. Wolsey.
Height, 1 ft 9 ins

21. CHAIR-TABLE, Early seventeenth century. From Mrs. Rees-Mogg, Clifford Manor, Gloucestershire.

Height, 3 ft 10 ins

22. SETTLE, with panelled back and base. Part of the seat forms a lid to the lower portion. Mid-seventeenth century. From the G. L. Riley Collection.

Height, 3 ft 11 ins   *Length*, 3 ft 2 ins

23. SETTLE, with panelled back and shaped sides. Part of the seat forms a lid to the lower portion. Early eighteenth century.

Height, 4 ft 4 ins
Length, 4 ft 8 ins

24. SETTEE, the seat, back, and adjustable panels above the arms covered with leather. Commonwealth period.

Height (to top of back), 3 ft 6 ins

25. SETTLE, of chestnut, the back and base panelled. Cupboards are fitted in the lower portion. Late seventeenth century. From Mrs. Rees-Mogg, Clifford Manor, Gloucestershire.

> *Height*, 7 ft 2 ins
> *Length*, 6 ft 2 ins

26. SETTEE, with panelled back surmounted by cresting of carved scrolls, and front legs tied by a carved stretcher. (The companion settee is dated 1715.) From Trinity College, Oxford.

27. ARMCHAIR, the back and seat covered with turkey work. First half of seventeenth century. From the Victoria and Albert Museum.

Height, 3 ft 2 ins
Width, 2 ft 4 ins

28. SETTEE, of beech (originally gilt) covered with crimson velvet, fastened to the frame with nails, and trimmed with a deep fringe. From Lord Sackville, Knole, Kent. *c.* 1610.

Height, 3 ft 5 ins
Length, 3 ft 8 ins

29. CUPBOARD, with enclosed lower stage and splay-fronted upper stage, mid-seventeenth century. From Mr. S. W. Wolsey.

Height, 4 ft 3 ins
Width, 4 ft

30. CUPBOARD, with open lower stage and splay-fronted upper stage. Early years of seventeenth century. From Brigadier W. Clark.

Height, 3 ft 10 ins
Width, 3 ft 11½ ins

31. COURT CUPBOARD, with baluster supports. The centre platform fitted with a drawer. *c.* 1635. From the James Thursby-Pelham Collection.

Height, 4 ft 2 ins
Length, 3 ft 11½ ins

32. COURT CUPBOARD with bulbous supports, the uppermost and centre platform fitted with a drawer. *c.* 1660. From the James Montagu Collection, Cold Overton Hall, Leicestershire.

Height, 4 ft
Width, 4 ft 6 ins

33. COURT CUPBOARD, of walnut (carved and inlaid) with carved cup and cover supports, and centre platform fitted with a drawer. From Sir Edward Barry, Bart., Ockwells, Berkshire.

Height, 4 ft
Length, 4 ft

34. COURT CUPBOARD, inlaid with geometrical patterns in dark and light woods, having lion masks applied to the columnar supports and drawer. From the G. L. Riley Collection.

Height, 3 ft 10½ ins
Width, 4 ft

Side table and bookcase

35. SIDE TABLE, with splayed sides, fitted with a cupboard. *c.* 1625. From the G. L. Riley Collection.

> *Height,* 2 ft 6 ins
> *Width,* 2 ft 11½ ins

36. PRESS or BOOKCASE, in two stages, the lower panelled, the upper glazed. *c.* 1660. From the James Thursby-Pelham Collection.

37. CUPBOARD, supported on fluted legs. (The masks form handles for the cupboard doors.) Early seventeenth century. From the James Thursby-Pelham Collection.

38. CUPBOARD (tridarn), in two stages surmounted by a canopy (Welsh type). Dated 1693. From Gwysaney, Flintshire.

39. TABLE (fitted with a drawer). *c.* 1675.
From the Adelaide Museum, Australia.

Height, 2 ft 5 ins
Width, 2 ft 6 ins

40. TABLE, with spiral-turned legs and
carved frieze. (Lancashire type), *c.* 1660–70.
From Browsholme Hall, Yorkshire.

Height, 2 ft 6 ins
Width, 2 ft 5¾ ins

41. TABLE, with fluted frieze and legs. Early seventeenth century. From the W. Simpson Collection.
Height, 2 ft 3½ ins   *Length*, 3 ft

42. DRAW TABLE of oak with legs of cup and cover form. (The top of elm.) Dated 1630. From Colonel N. R. Colville, Penheale, Cornwall.

Height, 2 ft 9 ins   *Length* (closed), 7 ft

43. GATE-LEG TABLE, with spiral legs and stretchers. Late seventeenth century. From Chetham's Hospital, Manchester.

Height, 2 ft 6 ins   *Length*, 7 ft 7 ins

44. TABLE, triangular, with a single gate-leg. From the Harold Peto Collection. Early seventeenth century.

Height, 2 ft 11¾ ins

45. TABLE, triangular, with a single gate-leg, the frame of fruitwood, the folding top of oak. From Mr. S. W. Wolsey.

Height, 2 ft 9 ins
Width, 3 ft

46. TABLE, drop-leaf. From the
W. Simpson Collection.

Height, 1 ft 9 ins

47. GATE-LEG TABLE, the legs headed with notched knobs. *c.* 1620. From
the W. Simpson Collection.

48. BED, carved and painted, the headboard and tester decorated with the arms of Cooper, Gilbert and other families. (Said to have come from Newton Mendip, Somerset.) First quarter of the seventeenth century. From Mrs. Rees-Mogg, Clifford Manor, Gloucestershire.

Height, 7 ft 2 ins *Length*, 7 ft

49. CHEST OF DRAWERS, with a lifting top. Late seventeenth century. From Lake House, Wiltshire.

Height, 2 ft 9½ ins
Length, 2 ft 10½ ins

50. CHEST OF DRAWERS, enriched with split spiral turnings, dated 1688. From Browsholme Hall, Yorkshire.

51. DRESSER, fitted with drawers and cupboards. Mid-seventeenth century. From the James Thursby-Pelham Collection.

Height, 2 ft 10½ ins   *Length*, 7 ft 1 in

52. DRESSER, fitted with drawers and cupboard. Early eighteenth century. From Mr. Leonard Knight.

Height, 2 ft 10 ins   *Length*, 6 ft

PART TWO

THE PERIOD OF WALNUT FURNITURE

Circa 1660–1720

I

HISTORICAL NOTE

AFTER the Restoration in 1660 the returning court brought in its train, not only a 'politer way of living', but influences from France and the Low Countries, which were seen in the new flamboyance that overlaid decoration and furniture. In a minor degree furniture reflected the 'loose and grandiloquent luxuries of the baroque'. The influence of France was spread not only by court fashion, but by the immigration of Huguenot craftsmen after the Revocation of the Edict of Nantes, refugees rich in trade secrets, energy and industrial skill, by whom certain industries such as silk weaving, and silversmiths' work gained an immense advantage.

The names of French carvers such as Robert Derignée and John Pelletier appear in the accounts of the Royal tradesmen in William III's reign; and even more widely influential was the architect and designer Daniel Marot who entered the service of William III and worked for him both in Holland and England. The marquetried furniture made by Gerriet Jensen for the Royal palaces is close to contemporary French work. The period was one of transition, in which the rich and profuse decoration of the late Stuart period was replaced by surface decoration.

New decorative processes came into fashion, such as veneering, marquetry, gesso and japanning. Accompanying these innovations there was a sudden renaissance of English craftsmanship, which is noted by John Evelyn[1] especially in the crafts of the smith and the joiner.

The reign of Anne is of interest on account of its revolutionary change in structure, following upon the introduction of a salient feature, the cabriole support. The cabriole which had a marked effect upon construction remained in favour, to the exclusion of almost every other type. The elimination of stretchers between the legs of chairs, couches, tables, and stands followed upon the introduction of the cabriole support. These remained absent in all designs until reintroduced on the square leg, about 1755.

[1] *Account of Architects and Architecture*, pp. 5-6.

The immediate ancestor of the cabriole was the form which was an adaptation of a quadruped's front leg from the knee downwards[1] and a goat's or deer's foot was at first generally used as a termination. In the seat furniture, the cabriole leg was accompanied by the curvature of the back.

A new range of articles of furniture witness to a rise in the standard of comfort of a settled society. Specialized pieces, hitherto rare or unknown, survive from the late seventeenth century and are listed in contemporary inventories. Among these may be mentioned long-case clocks, mirrors, day-beds, cabinets or presses with glazed doors, scrutoires and bureaux, and stands for lights. During the first quarter of the eighteenth century, specialized card tables, dressing glasses, tallboys (double chests of drawers) appear among the innovations.

[1] H. A. Tipping, *English Furniture of the Cabriole Period*, 1922, p. 4.

II

WOODWORK AND CONSTRUCTION

Walnut is a timber with a close even grain; soft to the tool and capable of fine polish. Its strength and stability is proved by its use for gunstocks, and for the propellers of aeroplanes. There are two varieties of walnut, *Juglans regia* (of which the timber is pale brown in colour, shaded with brown and marked with black veining); and *Juglans nigra* (black walnut) grown in Europe (especially in France and Italy) and in certain states of America (especially Virginia).

There was a considerable importation of black (Virginian) walnut into England in the early eighteenth century, and about 1720 a company was formed by the South Sea Company to import it from Virginia. The furniture made from this walnut in the solid is dark brown in colour and very similar to mahogany and can only be distinguished by examining a piece of freshly cut wood, which in the case of mahogany shows a red tinge.

There are records of the planting of English walnut (*Juglans regia*) in the late sixteenth and seventeenth centuries.

The conversion of walnut timber was similar to that of oak. In the best growths it is a hard and rather close-grained wood weighing about six pounds less per cubic foot than the average Cuban mahogany. Its chief disadvantage is the frequent flaws in the growth, which make it very difficult to obtain in large planks; also it is only wood near the centre of the tree (where the dark grain appears) that is of any value for furniture; towards the exterior the grain is very light and soft. It was rarely used in panelling, and except for legs and other short, solid members, was mostly cut into veneers. The timber of the trunks is generally straight-grained, and shows but little figure, and usually the stump is the only spot where a decided figure is found, at a point where the roots spread from the base of the tree. Burr wood veneers are obtained by slicing up the huge knots or burrs which form on a tree like great warts.

Veneering is defined as the method 'whereby several thin slices or leaves of fine wood of different sorts are applied and fastened on a ground of common

69

wood'. These slices or leaves were stated to be 'about a line thick', cut from blocks placed upright in a sawing press.[1]

Plain saw cut veneer was about one-sixteenth of an inch thick, but burr veneer was slightly thicker. Adhesion was obtained by means of glue. Before laying the veneer on the ground, the surface was toothed with a toothing plane. Veneer was usually laid with a special tool known as a veneering hammer; but after about 1690, for curved surfaces, a counterpart or mould of the surfaces, known as a caul, was accurately cut and shaped in another piece of wood, and (with a sheet of thin paper interposed to prevent sticking,) was heated and then clamped down upon the veneer until it had set. The caul and the hammer continued in use in eighteenth century. By the means of pressure by hammer or caul all surplus glue was forced from under the veneer. For narrow surfaces such as cross-banding, the veneering hammer was used, worked from the centre to the outside edges of the veneered surface.

Much skill was displayed in arranging the cuts to obtain the richest effects of the varying tones and lines in the grain, by matching, opposing, reversing successive sheets from the same block. In large areas (such as a table top, a fall front of a cabinet) 'quartering' or cutting four sheets from one block, and making a pattern by twice reversing the figure was usual. Pairing is produced by reversing two leaves from one block, and laying them with a single vertical or horizontal joint. Panel effects were obtained by bordering the veneered area with a cross-grained border. Pollard walnut is timber cut from the trees that have been subject to regular pollarding. Tiger walnut is a term applied to cuts from certain growths displaying dark, wavy stripes in the grain.

Oyster-shell veneer, or oyster pieces, were obtained by transverse cutting across the grain of small branches of walnut trees. These were arranged in sections. The markings of the rings gave the section an oyster-shell appearance, and the outer ring of pale sapwood was often included. During the late seventeenth century other figured woods, such as olive wood, maple, kingwood and laburnum were used as veneers.

Olive wood, a close-grained wood with a greenish yellow colour, with dark markings, which was imported from Italy, was used for parquetry during the late seventeenth century, and according to the *Treatise on Japanning and Varnishing* (1688) it was 'highly in request' for tables, stands and cabinets.

Laburnum is a wood of yellow tint, marked with brown streaks, which was used as parquetry veneer, especially during the early eighteenth century. King-

[1] *New and Universal Dictionary of Arts and Sciences* (1756).

DRAWER CONSTRUCTION.

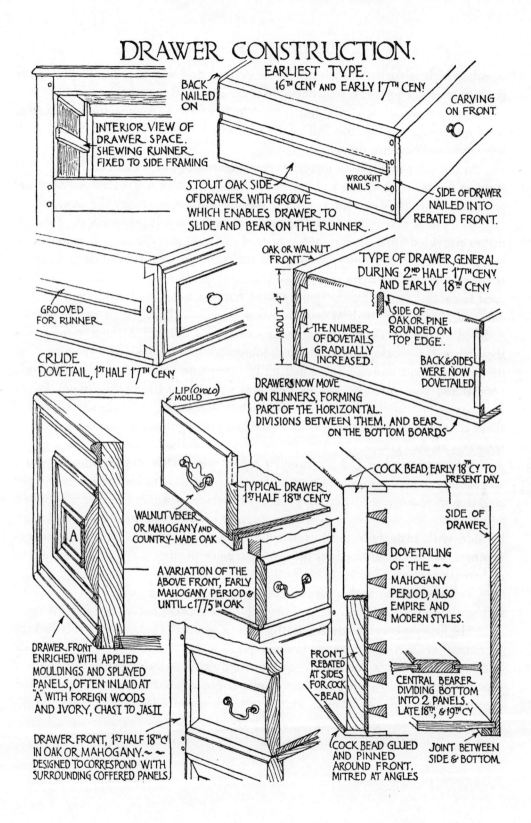

EARLIEST TYPE.
16TH CENY AND EARLY 17TH CENY.

BACK NAILED ON

CARVING ON FRONT.

INTERIOR VIEW OF DRAWER SPACE. SHEWING RUNNER FIXED TO SIDE FRAMING

STOUT OAK SIDE OF DRAWER WITH GROOVE WHICH ENABLES DRAWER TO SLIDE AND BEAR ON THE RUNNER.

WROUGHT NAILS

SIDE OF DRAWER NAILED INTO REBATED FRONT.

OAK OR WALNUT FRONT

TYPE OF DRAWER GENERAL DURING 2ND HALF 17TH CENY AND EARLY 18TH CENY.

ABOUT 4"

THE NUMBER OF DOVETAILS GRADUALLY INCREASED.

SIDE OF OAK OR PINE ROUNDED ON TOP EDGE.

BACK & SIDES WERE NOW DOVETAILED

GROOVED FOR RUNNER

CRUDE DOVETAIL, 1ST HALF 17TH CENY.

DRAWERS NOW MOVE ON RUNNERS, FORMING PART OF THE HORIZONTAL. DIVISIONS BETWEEN THEM, AND BEAR ON THE BOTTOM BOARDS

LIP (OVOLO) MOULD

COCK BEAD, EARLY 18TH CY TO PRESENT DAY.

TYPICAL DRAWER 1ST HALF 18TH CENY

WALNUT VENEER OR MAHOGANY AND COUNTRY-MADE OAK

SIDE OF DRAWER

DOVETAILING OF THE ~~ MAHOGANY PERIOD, ALSO EMPIRE AND MODERN STYLES.

A VARIATION OF THE ABOVE FRONT, EARLY MAHOGANY PERIOD & UNTIL c1775 IN OAK

A

DRAWER FRONT ENRICHED WITH APPLIED MOULDINGS AND SPLAYED PANELS, OFTEN INLAID AT "A" WITH FOREIGN WOODS AND IVORY, CHAS I TO JAS II

FRONT REBATED AT SIDES FOR COCK BEAD

CENTRAL BEARER DIVIDING BOTTOM INTO 2 PANELS. LATE 18TH & 19TH CY

DRAWER FRONT, 1ST HALF 18TH CY IN OAK OR MAHOGANY. ~~ DESIGNED TO CORRESPOND WITH SURROUNDING COFFERED PANELS.

COCK BEAD GLUED AND PINNED AROUND FRONT. MITRED AT ANGLES

JOINT BETWEEN SIDE & BOTTOM

wood, which is dark purplish-brown in colour, and was usually cut across the grain to show the figure, is very effective as veneer.

A native wood, yew, was much used in the form of veneer for furniture of good quality during the first half of the eighteenth century, and was liked for its fine figure and rich colouring.

In the oak period, both materials and methods of joiners and cabinet-makers were in the main identical, and both used oak and both constructed on the panel principle. With the development of the walnut this was no longer the case.

The joiner continued to use oak and frame his panels; whereas the cabinet-maker provided for flush surfaced veneered surfaces, and did not panel except in cases of structural necessity, such as the backs of carcases and the large doors of bookcases. Moreover, the use of oak was now much restricted; deal was often used in carcase work, but for parts taking friction wear, such as drawer linings, oak was always used in best work. A few large bookcases, such as the presses ordered by Samuel Pepys,[1] were made in oak and finished without veneer, but they were the work of architectural joiners rather than cabinet-makers. Oak proved a difficult base for the adhesion of veneer under changes of atmospheric conditions; consequently, yellow deal was substituted for carcase work in the majority of specimens. Pieces in solid walnut are usually of a darker tone, and there is not that transparency or life in the grain brought out in veneering, neither is there a marked grain.

Before the end of Queen Anne's reign it was evident that walnut furniture was subject to attack by wood-worm. This is considered to be one reason for the adoption of mahogany in the early Georgian period, yet many veneered cabinets and bureaux and solid work in walnut, such as chairs, continued to be made side by side with mahogany until well into the second quarter of the eighteenth century. Walnut continued to be used sparingly during the second half of the eighteenth century.

Veneered areas, such as doors and drawer fronts, were usually cross-banded and bordered with a narrow strip of herring-bone veneer, cut from striped wood.

The first veneered furniture, dating from Charles II's reign, invariably had the 'common' or 'through' dovetail in drawers, in which the end-grain is exposed on both sides of the angle formed by the front and sides. A more satisfactory method was the 'lapped'[2] dovetailing (which continued to be used through the eighteenth century). This type of dovetail was so called because a lap is left upon the pin

[1] Preserved in the Pepysian Library, Magdalene College, Cambridge.
[2] Also known as 'stopped' dovetail.

piece. In drawer work the dovetails are large and the 'pins' very narrow; in carcase dovetailing, the pins are cut larger where they were concealed.

After the Restoration, baluster forms were almost entirely supplanted for a few years by the twist on the frames of chairs, stools and tables. The wood-turning lathe in its plain form was incapable of turning shapes other than curves at right angles to the axis. According to the section dealing with turnery, in Moxon's *Mechanick Exercises, or The Doctrine of Handyworks*, a special contrivance was fitted on the wooden lathe when it was desired to cut shapes or mouldings obliquely to the axis of the work. It was termed swash turning—'you set it to that slope you intend the swash on your work shall have'—i.e. it was possible to regulate the frequency of the spiral. Moxon amplifies his directions by a woodcut, showing a twist-cut leg or baluster in the lathe. To turn a spiral to-day, a gear and slide rest are used. Some of the spirals are single, others 'two-start' or double—i.e. the tool has been started on its cutting in two separate places on the line or small moulding from which the spiral springs. Towards the close of the seventeenth century, the double twist was sometimes worked with two spirals quite separate and united only at cap and base of the stem. For this 'double open twist' the core was first bored out for the entire length, and the double twist was then begun on the lathe, and the hollows gouged out until the central hole was reached. The inner faces of each twist were carefully trimmed to give a circular section. Baluster turning revived during the late seventeenth century, but with the opening of the eighteenth century hand turning declined in favour.

In England the use of screws for securing metal fittings to the wood was practically unknown before the Restoration. In the second half of the seventeenth century the threads of screws were filed by hand, and the screw did not taper from the head downwards.[1]

Oil varnish was extensively used after the Restoration; and 'china varnish' (in which gum lac was the main ingredient) was also introduced. In this latter varnish, several coats were applied, and when dry, the surface was rubbed down, and the final coat polished by friction.

The late seventeenth century witnessed 'a brass monopoly' in mounts and handles, the metal, which lent itself to casting, was in keeping with the finished forms of post-Restoration furniture. Drawer handles were of peardrop or fantail shape, cast hollow and attached to a circular or star-shaped plate, the handle being attached to a double strip of brass or iron, which was passed through a small hole in the drawer front, then parted, pressed down, and the ends turned over and driven into the wood.

[1] The screw with gimlet-pointed head first appeared at the Great Exhibition (1851).

The escutcheon usually took the form of a cartouche of irregular oval form, with the keyhole pierced on the smooth central field which was surrounded by cast decoration. The solid back plate of handles was often engraved; in the reign of George I, the brass plate was shaped by cutting out the centre in various patterns. The key escutcheons of the early years of the eighteenth century were similar in shape to the back plates of the handles, except in the case of escutcheons required for a narrow space on clock cases and the doors of cupboards.

The drawer-handle dating from the early eighteenth century took the form of a cast loop or ring handle. A form dating from about 1720 is a plain ring hanging from the centre of a circular disc or back-plate which was fixed to the drawer by two tangs (or strips) of brass threaded through the plate and bent out against the back of the drawer. The loop handle also was at first fixed by brass tangs, but this fixing was superseded by the suspension of the handle from a socket on the inner side of the fixing bolts (which were held in place by a nut at the inner end).

III

MARQUETRY

SHORTLY after the Restoration there was a development of marquetry as a surface enrichment distinct in technique from inlay in mother of pearl in fashion during the second half of the seventeenth century. The art was no doubt introduced from France, and there are several contemporary pieces of furniture[1] in which floral sprays are relieved against contrasting grounds. Evelyn as early as 1664 mentions in his *Sylva* the varieties of exotic woods used by inlayers, and the shading of certain portions of wood by dipping a section into a pan of hot sand.[2]

Marquetry appears upon fine specimens of walnut-veneered chests of drawers, cabinets, bureaux, tables, chairs, and mirror frames, during a period of nearly fifty years (from about 1665 to 1715). Certain details of construction such as good dovetailing in place of lapping and housing joints, stamp the native production. English marquetry was invariably applied on flat surfaces in cabinet work, while the Dutch *marqueteurs* delighted in laying their work on surfaces of concave and convex section.

In the reigns of Charles II and James II designs consisted of either foliage in large scrolling patterns, in two shades of brown, or floral designs, consisting of sprays of tulips, carnations, lilies, anemones and other flowers, sometimes grouped in a vase, or issuing from formal arrangements of acanthus foliage. Instances of dated pieces in which the design is of scrolling foliage is a cabinet in the Victoria and Albert Museum (1688), and a press made for James, Duke of York.

Birds are frequently introduced in floral marquetry; but human figures are of rare occurrence. In the Victoria and Albert Museum there is a cabinet (dated 1688) in which the door of the interior cupboard[3] is marquetried with a figure on horseback and an attendant; and a profile head within a medallion appears on the cresting of a mirror at Ham House.

[1] e.g. Furniture from the Chateau de Montargis in the Victoria and Albert Museum.
[2] *Sylva*, Chapter XXXI, 35.
[3] W. 14-1911.

Early in the eighteenth century the scale of the design was reduced; and the flowers and birds were omitted, and foliage was rendered in spiky and scrolling patterns closely spaced and interwoven, resembling stylized 'seaweed' or 'endive'.

A different type of marquetry is the simple geometrical kind. It generally consisted of interlacing and tangential circles of narrow lines of sycamore or holly; or of fan and star shapes. With this type the ground was generally veneered in oyster wood, but other veneers, such as yew tree, plane tree, pear tree, laburnum, and burr elm, were employed.

Marquetry-cutting in veneer is a skilled craft. A variety of tints was obtained by dyeing portions of the wood; by introducing sections of ebony, pearl, and ivory; and also by scorching wood with hot sand. The design was first drawn upon paper, duplicates being made by pricking through; the pattern was then pasted on the topmost of two or more sheets of veneer which were held together with panel pins, or by glued paper interposed. The marquetry-cutter then worked along the lines of the drawing with a fine frame saw. Portions of each layer were selected, and after any requisite staining, were arranged in the spaces on the ground, then held together by gluing a sheet of paper over the whole. After roughening its under side and the surface to be veneered, it was glued down upon the carcase. The hot caul was next applied and clamped down, or placed in the press for about twenty-four hours.

Another method was that in which the pattern was cut away from the ground layer, which was then glued in position, and out of another layer of contrasting tint (also marked or covered with the design) the ornament was cut out and glued into the gaps waiting for their reception in the previously cut and fixed 'ground'. This needed greater skill but ensured close joints. When thoroughly set, all paper and superfluous glue would be scraped and sanded off.

In each layer half would be used and half discarded; these seconds or 'negative' portions were sometimes used in the panels of another piece of furniture, and examples are extant in which the patterns are identical, the only difference being that the light parts of one are dark on another, and vice versa.

Illustrations on pages 113 and 114.

IV

JAPANNING

ORIENTAL lacquer in the form of cabinets and screens was introduced into Europe by the East India Companies during the reign of Charles II, and such cabinets mounted on carved and gilt stands were found in great country houses built, altered, or furnished from the Restoration to the death of Queen Anne. An imitative craft, japanning, was started with much success, and was practised both by skilled japanners and by amateurs. By 1688, the desire for instruction warranted the issue of a treatise by Stalker and Parker *On Japanning and Varnishing* illustrated by 'above a hundred distinct patterns', and their work was followed by William Salmon's *Polygraphice* in which the earlier treatise is freely plagiarized.

At the date of the issue of Stalker and Parker's treatise there were two varieties of lacquer imitated; the Chinese incised lacquer (known as 'Bantam work') and lacquer with painted gilt and raised decoration applied to the ground. In English imitation of Chinese incised lacquer, a ground was laid consisting of several coats of a mixture of size and whiting; and the design afterwards cut out of this ground, coloured and gilded.

Japanning with decoration in gilding, paint and relief was in its initial stages very similar to gesso work, the ground and the portions in relief being obtained by bodying up with whiting and size. After the priming was dry, several coats of coloured varnish formed the ground. Recipes given in the *Treatise* (1688) show a wide range of colour, but surviving examples have usually a black, and, more rarely, a red ground. The design was painted on this ground in colours mixed with gum arabic, and gilding. Raised details were added by dropping a paste of whiting and gum arabic on to the surface. The raised detail, when set were shaped, coloured and gilded. Designs which frequently occur are an outdoor scene of Chinese character with a pavilion, figures, and distant mountains, and figures of birds, and sprays of flowering shrubs. There is a tendency, in the words of a treatise on japanning, to 'spread the surface pretty equal'.

Japanning, from its fragility, has suffered from wear and tear, and the denting and scratching of the surface is very noticeable in unrestored pieces. Many objects were finished in japanning, such as cabinets, bureaux, bookcases, chests, mirrors and dressing glasses.

Illustrations on page 115.

V

CHAIRS

THE chairs of the walnut period are divided into (1) those of the late Stuart period in which solid walnut is used in construction, and the carving and type is somewhat similar to contemporary Dutch and French chairs, and (2) chairs of the cabriole period, characterized by the curvature of the legs and back in which walnut veneer was used on the back and seat-rail. There is no transitional type between these two forms.

After the Restoration the twist or spiral is found in conjunction with the other types of turning. Some of these twists are cut very hollow and appear irregular.

In the years immediately following the Restoration all legs, stretchers, and back uprights were twist turned. All these members were out of a square section, and rectangular portions were left for the mortice and tenon joints by which they were framed together. The back uprights (terminating in knob finials), which are continuations of the rear legs, sloped backwards to give added comfort, thereby forming an angle where the upright rises above the seat. This rake became more pronounced until (*circa* 1680-1690) it was in some instances excessive. The angle was a weak point, except in armchairs. If single chairs be examined, it will be found that the direction of the grain of the wood is parallel with a straight line drawn between the top finial and the foot. In this way the danger of short grain at the bend was partly overcome. The rails of the back (which at first were devoid of any cresting) and also the seat frame, were of rectangular section, sometimes lightly moulded on the edge, and were holed to receive the cane panel, which in early specimens was of large mesh.

Arms were at first quite flat, bowed on plan, and tenoned into the back uprights and to an upward extension of the front legs. The feet were usually circular, turned in vase or ball form. In some chairs vertical slats filled the back in lieu of caning.

The seat frame was frequently incised with a lozenge or lattice pattern on the outer faces. Carving formed an important part in the design; the front stretcher

79

fixed half-way up the legs, was a flat member four or five inches wide, on which simplified acanthus leaves centring in a flat-petalled rose or crown were carved; this same *motif* appears on the top and bottom rails of the back, and also in many cases on the inner uprights to which the caning was laced at the sides. The carving was varied with cherubs supporting a crown or basket of fruit and flowers, and was in relief against a background.[1] The rectangular surfaces at the joints were carved in slight relief, and in some chairs the front legs were shaped and carved in tall scroll form instead of twist turning, which was still popular for the rest of the framing. Almost immediately after the appearance of the scrolled front legs, simple baluster turning reappeared on many chairs for back uprights and side and rear stretchers.

The arms which were of rounded section (of the same section as the scrolled legs) and shaped to a hollow downward curve, were finished with a large scroll over the front supports with leafage carved in slight relief. These scrolled ends tended to curve outward, becoming more extravagant in material; their supports above the seat frame were often also scroll shaped. The mesh of the caning became closer in the last decade of the century. The outlines of the carving on front stretchers and back cresting were no longer restrained within parallel limits, and with the addition of S scrolls and other detail (often foliated), they rose in height at the centre. The cresting was still between and framed into the sides of the uprights. In some chairs possessing these features, the back is filled with about three splats of carved and opposed S scrolls arranged in groups and tiers.

The seat frame was composed of four separate members mortised into the sides of the legs, and a running leaf design was frequently carved on the exposed surfaces. The space devoted to caning in the back was reduced and the preference for scrolled carved forms (or simple turning) dominated the legs, many being not far removed from the cabriole shape.

The open-back chairs of James II were taller and narrower than the types of Charles II's reign. Many chairs had stuffed backs and seats, the covering materials being needlework, damask, or velvet, trimmed with rich fringes.

Scrolled legs were also designed for single chairs, without any square portion at the top into which the seat members could be tenoned; the seat was, accordingly, framed up separately, then let into the back uprights and onto the front legs, having a hole bored at each front corner into which the turned and tapered top

---

[1] The motif of *putti* supporting a crown is generally associated with the Restoration period, but it continued in use as late as 1697, when Thomas Roberts sent in an account for 'Twelve chairs carved boys and crowns'.

of the leg could fit like a dowel, and a peg was often driven in the side of the seat frame for greater security. This was, however, a defective method compared with tenoning into mortices in the legs. On these seat frames, which are broad and thin, a round mould is generally found on the outer faces.

The scrolled leg and carved stretcher did not completely oust turning on these front members, for about 1690 chairs appeared with a swell-turned leg, and a double-swell or a carved stretcher; legs also were given a sudden broadening like an inverted cup and the foot was spread. In some cases there was the carved 'Spanish' foot. Other terminations were various types of moulded arch forms, sometimes carved with foliage in full relief.

In some types, the cresting, only slightly carved, rode over the uprights and often partook of the moulded form of the arched stretcher; also the tall and narrow caned panel has a moulded uncarved frame, with top and bottom often rounded or ogee shaped. An exceptional type influenced by French design is described as the 'Marot' chair. In this the space between the uprights is filled with rich pierced carving composed of foliage, opposed scrolls and French *motifs* such as the *lambrequin*, and is capped by an ornate cresting, which is repeated in the front stretcher. The stretcher in some cases was not attached to the front legs, but set back a few inches and tenoned to the side stretchers at the lower level. There is much variation in the legs of 'Marot' chairs, particularly the front pair, where turning is less usual than square moulded and geometrically shaped forms. A broad inverted cup (either circular or octagonal) tapered to a small section over the rectangular block at the stretcher level, and again extended to an octagonal or a bun foot, is frequently found. The faces of the square cutting were often slightly sunk in panels. The seat was deep framed and stuffed over.

During the last years of the seventeenth century many chairs have serpentine stretchers, which are arranged diagonally. They are framed into the block immediately above the foot; and the cross-brace stretchers are of a delicate moulded section and are usually lap-halved where they cross or tenon into a central block, the former joint being secured with a peg which is utilized as a fixing for a turned finial. These graceful stretchers are useless as constructional ties. This leg bracing is only to be found on fine chairs.

Many country-made Stuart high-back chairs had rush seats, as cane was not obtainable everywhere, nor would it stand hard wear like the rush. The backs of such chairs were generally filled with arrangement of narrow slats. Simple turning characterized the legs, but the arched cresting and stretcher were often essayed. Chairs were often made of beech, coloured or painted black.

With the advent of the cabriole the back uprights were curved backwards in serpentine form—i.e. they were convex just above the seat, and then became concave towards the top rail. An arched cresting rode over these uprights, and a wide shaped splat, at first pierced, filled the central space, being framed to bottom rail and cresting. At first only the front legs were cabriole, and were often without shoulder-pieces. There were three shaped stretchers, one on each side from front to back, and a cross-member joining them about midway. The rear legs were square for the most part or plain turned, and ended in a club foot. The cabriole curve was very decided, and the foot was at first hoof-shaped (the *pied-de-biche*). The seat was deep framed, and generally stuffed over. The shaping of a cabriole leg is one of the few operations which must still be done largely by hand. First, a suitable length of walnut (or, later, mahogany) was selected for closeness of grain and freedom from all faults and shakes. For a chair leg it might be three inches square and about eighteen inches long. On two adjacent sides of this piece the outline curves would be marked, probably from a thin wooden template. The top or knee curves would appear about three inches from an end of the wood to allow of the necessary block into which the mortices would be cut to receive the tenons of the seat rails. The next operation was to clamp one end in the bench, and with a large bow-saw cut the profiles marked on the wood. The result was a curved leg of rectangular section, and it should be noted that several examples were made in which the legs were left in square cabriole form. For the usual form, however, the next step was first to place the leg in a lathe and turn the pad foot (unless it was intended to carve a hoof), and then again to fix in the bench and with a spokeshave and rasp to reduce the arrises to a rounded section, leaving it rough on the knee if carving was intended there. The leg was now complete, except that on either side of the knee there was an abrupt finish on a vertical face; this, as some specimens show us, was so left, on others the shape was rounded off with an applied acorn knob or turned rosette, but generally (particularly in the later work) a shoulder-piece was dowelled or merely glued on at each side, partaking of a continuation of the leg curve and shaped on its under side. This has the effect of supporting the seat rail, but does little more than strengthen against racking. The chair back, which hitherto had been contained between two parallel uprights, now became spoon-shaped, with an S curve on the side uprights and a vase-shaped splat in the central space. Those parallel vertical lines which had hitherto enclosed the form of the back were rarely found in the full cabriole period, and a shoulder is formed on the uprights a few inches above the seat; above that the uprights together provided a hoop-shaped back, which was completed by an

DEVELOPMENT OF THE CABRIOLE LEG. c.1695-1760.

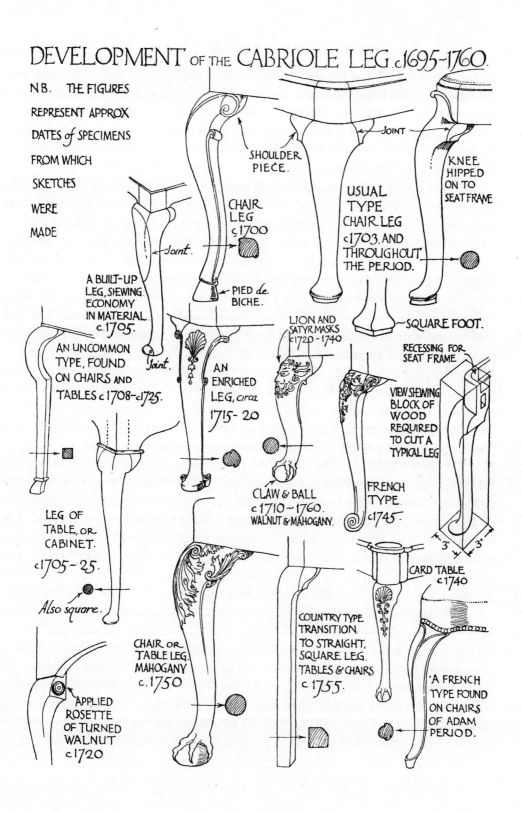

NB. THE FIGURES REPRESENT APPROX DATES of SPECIMENS FROM WHICH SKETCHES WERE MADE

SHOULDER PIECE.

JOINT

KNEE HIPPED ON TO SEAT FRAME

CHAIR LEG. c1700

Joint.

A BUILT-UP LEG, SHEWING ECONOMY IN MATERIAL. c.1705.

PIED de BICHE.

USUAL TYPE CHAIR LEG c1703, AND THROUGHOUT THE PERIOD.

SQUARE FOOT.

AN UNCOMMON TYPE, FOUND ON CHAIRS AND TABLES c1708-c1725.

Joint.

AN ENRICHED LEG, circa 1715-20

LION AND SATYR MASKS c1720-1740

RECESSING FOR SEAT FRAME

VIEW SHEWING BLOCK OF WOOD REQUIRED TO CUT A TYPICAL LEG

LEG OF TABLE, OR CABINET. c1705-25.

Also square.

CLAW & BALL c1710-1760. WALNUT & MAHOGANY.

FRENCH TYPE. c1745.

3"   3"

CARD TABLE c1740

CHAIR OR TABLE LEG. MAHOGANY c.1750

APPLIED ROSETTE OF TURNED WALNUT c1720

COUNTRY TYPE TRANSITION TO STRAIGHT, SQUARE LEG. TABLES & CHAIRS c1755.

A FRENCH TYPE FOUND ON CHAIRS OF ADAM PERIOD.

arched cresting bar; the moulded front faces of the uprights were carried across the latter without break, and also across a connecting rail a few inches above the seat; the splat, framed into the cresting bar and this lower rail, was narrower than the first model and had a more definite outline which somewhat resembled a fiddle. The stretchers were little altered; the seat was sometimes stuffed over, but usually rested on a drop-in frame.

A number of chairs dating from the early eighteenth century were entirely without stretchers, and these fell out of use until revived between the square legs in mahogany chairs. Their rejection necessarily put all the strain into the joints with the seat frame; but seat rails were sufficiently deep and tenoned into the vertical block left at the top of the leg above the knee. The upper part of this block and the seat rails were reduced in thickness to admit of a separate drop-in seat. To strengthen the joints between legs and seat rails, triangular blocks were screwed into the four angles, and often utilized as a bearing for the seat. The seat framing had a small quadrant mould round the top edge, and the lower edge was sometimes shaped to balancing curves. In the seat frame the two front corners often were rounded, i.e. the block forming the top of the leg followed the rounded surface made by reducing the arris on the knee; and shortly afterwards the front rail was bowed, concave, or serpentine, and the side rails were also serpentine or straight on plan, converging towards the back. The finest specimens had the seat framing, the back uprights and the splat veneered with figured walnut.

The splat united the shaped top rail of the back to the seat frame; also, like the uprights, it was carefully shaped to fit the spinal curves; it rose from a shaped shoe-piece planted on the rear seat rail, and was usually profiled in balanced curves up to the top rail, into which it was tenoned. Generally it was not pierced, but examples exist in which it forks at the top, to enter the head rail at two separate points. Armchairs were made to match the various types of single chairs, and departed from the earlier traditions in that the arm supports rose from the side rails of the seat a few inches back. They were in rare cases a continuation of the front legs.

The arms and supports were for the most part of rounded section, serpentine in rising to their full height, then bowed and dished in the horizontal part, taken back and framed into the uprights. Others (generally later examples) rode over the support, and finished in a carved scroll or volute. On a few fine examples the splat had delicate leaf carving on its edges, on others it was inlaid with marquetry, which also appeared on the front seat rail. In examples enriched with carving upon veneered splats and rails the pieces of walnut were glued down on to the veneer and then carved, the junction being so perfect as almost to avoid detection.

With the hoop back the vertical plain uprights were again revived, but they were more slender and of purely round section above the seat; they were also rather tall, and the junction with the top rail is, in some cases, a right angle with the corners rounded off. On these chairs the splat is often of very plain outline. Upholstered chairs were of two types: (1) the winged armchair with cabriole legs often connected by thin stretchers, and with a broad and high back, fitted with wing-pieces and scroll-over arms; (2) single chairs upholstered on back and seat, and showing no woodwork except the cabriole legs.

Illustrations on pages 116-123.

VI

STOOLS

STOOLS were still largely used for seating during the second half of the seven-teenth century, and the furnishing accounts for the Royal palaces under William III show that for every chair half a dozen high stools and forms were provided, an indication of their ceremonial use.

They generally had upholstered seats of rectangular or circular form, and their supports reproduced the various turned and shaped legs and stretchers of contemporary chairs. In some cases, however, the stool has a wooden seat sunk for a squab cushion. The rails were covered with the upholstery material, but in the early eighteenth century the seat was movable, fitting into the frame.

Illustrations on pages 124 and 125.

VII

DAY-BEDS AND SETTEES

THE settee or couch,[1] which had been known for some years prior to the Restoration, had framing resembling contemporary chairs. With the introduction of caning, the day-bed, an elongated caned stool on six or more legs with corresponding stretchers, became fashionable. At one end the two legs continue up, very much cranked at the seat block to form a sloping support. This end had either a fixed caned panel, or one hinged by wooden dowels between its bottom rail and the side uprights. With the hinged panel secured by cords or chains at the top, the angle was adjustable. The sloping back was not structurally sound, since a strain was thrown on the cross grain of the uprights.

The caned day-bed did not strictly need a cover or cushion, but its use without a cover would have speedily destroyed the cane. When the cane was covered, there was no need for such a fragile seat, and method of lacing and trussing was substituted. The day-bed followed the evolutions of the chair; during William III's reign it was upholstered, and the head rest became a fixture. The supports were usually of the tapered baluster form which took the place of the scroll-shaped leg.

The settee was a wider version of the high-backed, upholstered chair with padded arms. During the cabriole period the hoop-back chair was used as a model for a novel type of settee formed by linking two or three chair backs with arms at each end. Cabriole legs also appeared under the seat rail immediately in front of the back supports. The back members and the seat rails of these settees are usually found overlaid with veneer and the top rail and the edges of the splats were often carved. The arms ended in scrolls or in bird or animal heads; and the cabriole legs were carved with the escallop shell and husk on the knees. The feet finished in claw and ball, or were turned in pad shape. Stretchers are known on some specimens.

Illustrations on pages 126 and 127.

---

[1] The usual term for the day-bed in the late seventeenth century and early eighteenth century was the 'couch'. Pepys bought in 1666 'a set of chairs and couch'.

VIII

TABLES

T HE twist turning of the Restoration is used on the legs and stretchers of tables, though simple turning still persisted. The description of the earlier oak models applies to those of the second half of the seventeenth century, with the exception that the trestle type was almost at an end.

Twist turning persisted longer on the legs of tables than on chairs, and during the reigns of James II and William III many specimens were made in which the twist rises above a vase form, and the spiral is graduated. The vase form was also used when the twist was not employed, and is then found in conjunction with well-proportioned contrasting curves, one member of these frequently being the inverted cup shape. Many of these post-Restoration tables had their flap hinges secured with screws, though the nail was still commonly used on country-made specimens. The central portion of the top was still secured with dowel pegs.

Gate-leg tables were used for meals, and many were of large dimensions and fitted with four gates; others were made as two distinct semi-circular units, which could be butted together or pulled apart to admit of the insertion of a rectangular central table (also on a gated frame). This last portion with gates shut would, when not in use, form a narrow side table. The large and the very small tables are now rare, the latter being the most sought after.

To prevent the top boards of small models appearing too thick, they were generally splayed back on the under side around the edge. Some specimens of gate tables made about 1700 followed the fashion of many side and centre tables in having flat-shaped stretchers, the gate hinges being formed in the wood where the dowel pivot was not applicable. Soon after the Restoration, legs and stretchers were twist-turned; then there followed a vogue for baluster turned legs to which the flat-shaped cross stretchers were added. On certain tables of very small dimensions and light construction the cross stretchers were delicate, and much like those of moulded section on contemporary chairs. But on those of more usual size (about three feet or more wide), the stretchers were generally designed on a different principle. Firstly, they were larger and of plain flat section (about

COMPARATIVE EXAMPLES OF TURNING. 1600~1800.

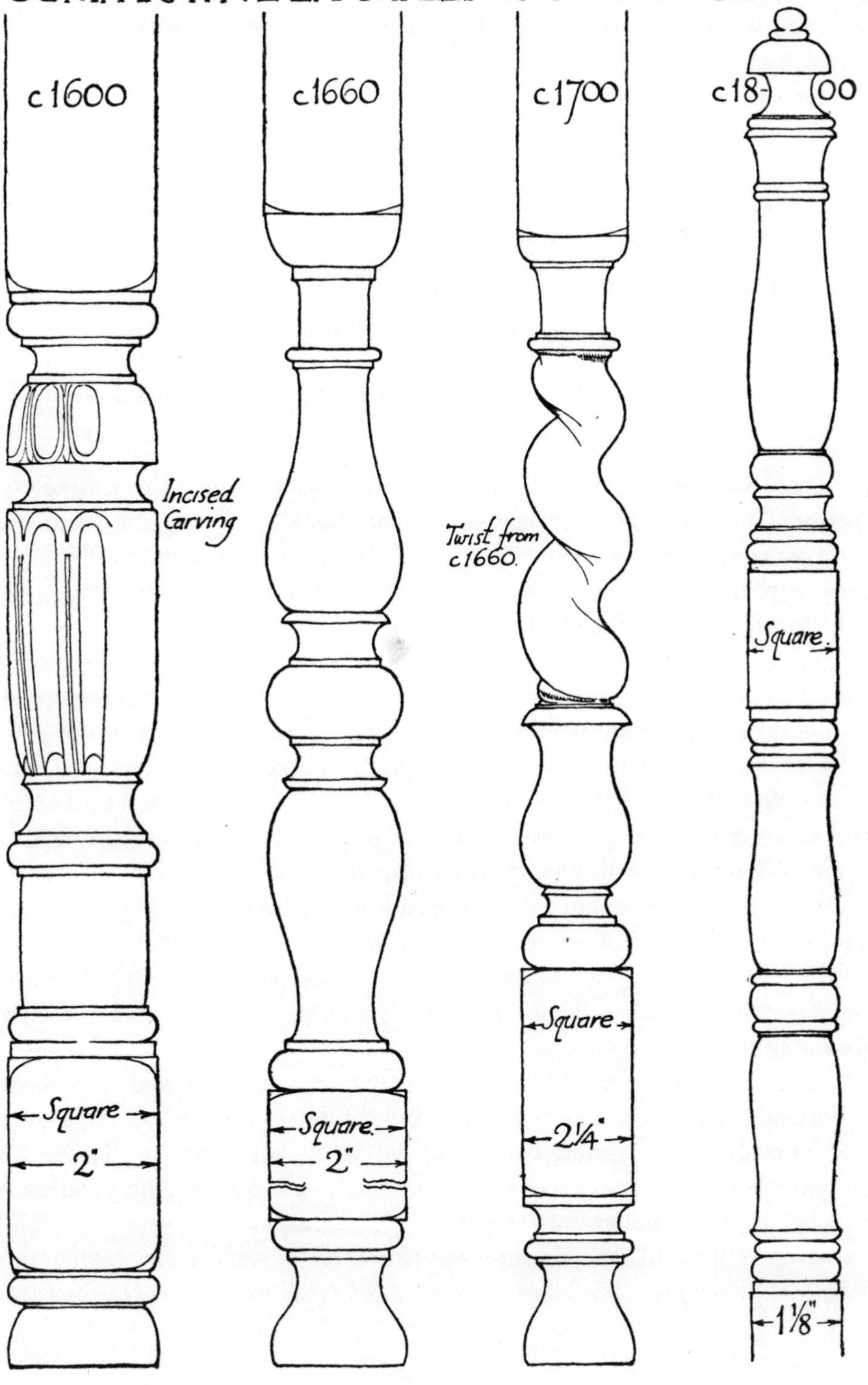

c 1600

c 1660

c 1700

c 18—   00

Incised Carving

Twist from c 1660.

Square

← Square →
2"

← Square →
2"

← Square →
2¼"

← 1⅛ →

three inches wide and one inch thick), and at their extremities broadened out into a flat square, which was utilized as a seating for the leg. There were three general types:

(a) The serpentine curved cross with a finial at the cross-over.

(b) A Y-shape at each end of the stretcher connected by a central shelf of circular or oval form.

(c) A reversion to the older plan of four stretchers, running from leg to leg, but with the square widening under each leg where they were lap-halved; for the distance between the legs the inner and outer edges of these stretchers were shaped in convex, concave, and ogee curves.

In conformity with the table top and the main under frame these three types of stretchers were frequently veneered in cross-banded walnut; also, they were built up as a separate unit, a central hole being bored through the flat square corners or extremities, which accommodated a large dowel to unite the leg with a ball-turned foot and thereby fix the stretcher frame.

The top, which was dowel fixed, had its surface veneered in one piece or quartered with cross-banded borders, sometimes with feather or herring-bone inlay. The projecting edge would be thumb moulded (now termed an ovolo mould), which would be worked in cross-grain walnut. The frieze of the under frame (excepting tables designed for a central position), was usually fitted with one or two drawers, constructed with dovetailing in oak or deal linings, and veneered with walnut on the front to match the top.

Tables, apparently designed for dressing or writing, were frequently constructed with a much deeper frieze, the lower edge of which was shaped in graceful curves balancing about the centre, at which point it became narrowest. These curves were usually edged with a tiny projecting bead, similar to the cock bead on drawer edges.

In the centre part of the frieze a shallow drawer was fitted, and on each side, two short drawers, one above the other, or one deep drawer. The edges of the drawer openings were generally surrounded by a half-round or double reed mould, following the practice of design on chests of drawers. The practice still obtained of fitting the upper drawers tight under the top.

During William III's reign some ornamental tables were made, having square or octagonal cut and moulded legs with moulded cross stretchers. During the last

FOLDING FRAMES, GATES, & BRACKETS; ON 18TH CY TABLES.

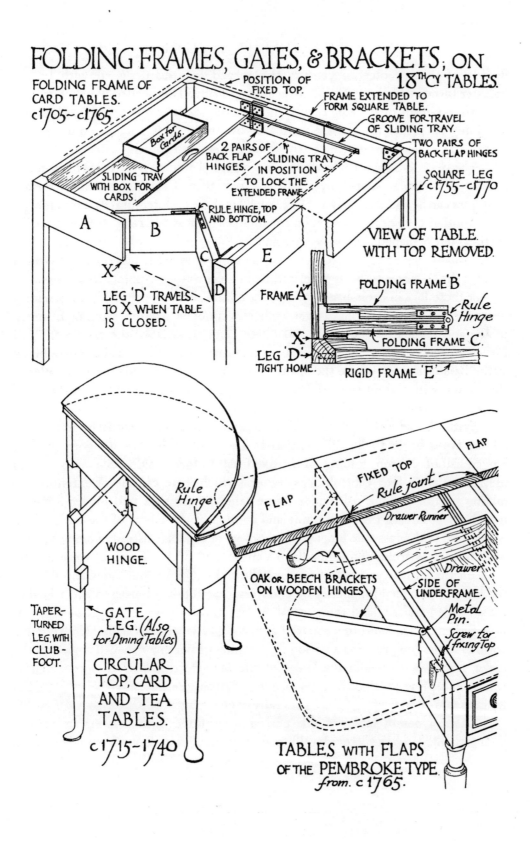

FOLDING FRAME OF CARD TABLES.
c1705~c1765

POSITION OF FIXED TOP.

FRAME EXTENDED TO FORM SQUARE TABLE.

GROOVE FOR TRAVEL OF SLIDING TRAY.

Box for Cards.

2 PAIRS OF BACK FLAP HINGES.

SLIDING TRAY IN POSITION TO LOCK THE EXTENDED FRAME.

TWO PAIRS OF BACK FLAP HINGES

SQUARE LEG c1755-c1770

SLIDING TRAY WITH BOX FOR CARDS.

RULE HINGE, TOP AND BOTTOM.

A   B

C

X

E

LEG 'D' TRAVELS TO X WHEN TABLE IS CLOSED.

D

VIEW OF TABLE WITH TOP REMOVED.

FRAME 'A'

FOLDING FRAME 'B'

Rule Hinge

X

LEG 'D' TIGHT HOME.

FOLDING FRAME 'C'

RIGID FRAME 'E'

Rule Hinge

WOOD HINGE.

FLAP

FIXED TOP
Rule joint

FLAP

Drawer Runner

OAK OR BEECH BRACKETS ON WOODEN HINGES

Drawer

SIDE OF UNDERFRAME.

Metal Pin.

Screw for fixing Top

TAPER-TURNED LEG, WITH CLUB-FOOT.

GATE LEG. (Also for Dining Tables)

CIRCULAR TOP, CARD AND TEA TABLES.

c1715-1740

TABLES WITH FLAPS OF THE PEMBROKE TYPE.
from c1765.

decade of the seventeenth century the turned leg was designed with bolder baluster forms, and also with the inverted cup shape. This needed wood of greater breadth to permit of it being turned in the solid, and to avoid waste was built up by gluing on pieces to take the 'cup', or by turning this portion on a separate member and then dowelling on to the thinner member beneath.

The twist legs appear in varied forms as a spiral column over a vase or an upper and lower twist, separated by a ball and reel turned centre, which in certain examples can be dated as early as 1675. Such legs have architectural base mouldings.

Another type of leg appears on small tables from about 1675. It was of square section, but S shaped, ending at top and base in a plain scroll outline. Such legs were usually placed to face outwards at an angle somewhat less than 45°, which enables the S curves to be appreciated from a central view-point. It was usual to veneer these legs in cross-banding, and they were often enriched with marquetry when the top was so treated. The stretchers were of flat section, running from leg to leg and shaped on the inner and outer faces. Invariably the feet were ball turned. A few of this type, apparently of English construction, had a square block at the base of the leg where the stretchers were connected. Many small tables at this period with walnut veneered tops and stretchers had turned legs in the more durable solid yew.

With the adoption of the cabriole leg, which was peculiarly suitable to tables, types begin to be differentiated. The card table was designed with a hinged half of the top, folding on the fixed half to form a side table when not in use. There were four cabriole legs, two of which were capable of extension on folding portions of the oak under frame; there were thus two hinges for each movable leg, one on the fixed frame and another at the elbow of the fold, which were fitted with brass rule hinges. The corners of the top, instead of being square, were formed as projecting segments of a circle, and circles in walnut were slightly sunk on the surface as positions for candlesticks. On all four sides an elliptical sinking was provided for money or counters. The top was bordered and edged in cross-banded walnut, and the general surface usually covered in green cloth or velvet glued down and often secured at the edges with brass nails. The rounded corners of the top provided a reason for forming projecting rounded angles on the under frame, with which the knees of the legs were shaped to agree. These tables, excepting those of country origin, wherein the necessary balance on the leg curves is often wanting, were generally of charming proportions.

Other types of tables of this period were fitted with drawers in various arrangements, and the later developments in mouldings around the edges again corresponded with contemporary work on chests of drawers. Tables with a top of solid wood were probably being intended as wash-stands. The moulded edge of the top was either the large ovolo (as on earlier specimens) or had one of much less width, confined almost to the top edge, and turned in at the corners.

Illustrations on pages 128, 129 and 144.

IX

BUREAUX AND BOOKCASES

D URING the third quarter of the seventeenth century bureaux of various forms were designed.

The drop front secretaire or cabinet (scrutoire) which was copied in this country from Continental examples, continued in use during the early eighteenth century. The great majority of surviving examples date from between 1665 and 1710. In some instances the drop front cabinet is mounted on a chest of drawers, but there are rare examples of open stands as a base with turned or spirally twisted legs. Early in William III's reign the bureau made its appearance. The first models were a utilization of the small side table and gate-leg table combined, upon which was placed a box having a large flap at a flat angle, and containing small drawers and pigeon-holes. The flap was hinged and swung forward to be supported upon the tops of the two gate legs.

In the last years of the seventeenth century followed the bureau on chest, in which the flap-covered compartment rested on the top of a chest of drawers with occasionally a central knee-hole. At the base there was a projecting plinth mould and feet either of the corner bracket type or turned in ball and bun forms. A characteristic of early examples of this type is the oversailing of the bureau portion over the base. They ranged in width from about two feet three inches to three feet six inches. The knee-hole type was also made with flat table top, under which a writing slide was fitted. When the flap became steeper, the space inside was more elaborately worked out in shaping the fronts and divisions of the small drawers and pigeon-holes. A small central cupboard was usual, enriched with side pilasters, behind which a secret compartment was frequently contrived. The drawer fronts and mouldings followed the design of those on chests of drawers, and the flap was enriched with veneered border strips and surrounding moulding. There was another type of small bureau, about two feet wide, in which the box with sloping flap was mounted upon four legs of tapered and turned section, generally tied by flat veneered stretchers. In the early eighteenth century these rested on cabriole legs. These small bureaux (which are very scarce) date between 1690 and 1730. It was usual to veneer the entire inner surface of the flap, but some examples were faced with a panel of green velvet.

The walnut bureaux in two stages was common in the homes of well-to-do people from the reign of James II until about 1745. In this, the bureau with drawers beneath is surmounted by a cornice either straight, domed, or pedimented. In the double-domed design, the cupboard doors are also arched. Throughout the age of walnut, these doors were usually faced with mirror glass, bevelled at the edges. The fittings of the upper stage vary in detail, but a central cupboard flanked by tall partitions for ledgers is usual.

From about 1700 the bureau top became united to its supporting chest of drawers, though many retained the applied or 'planted' moulding fixed around the body a few inches below the hinges of the sloping flap, which had originally covered the joint. The space within at this level was utilized as a well, to which access was gained by lifting or sliding a portion of the back part of the writing surface. There were at least two methods of supporting the flap when pulled forward into a horizontal position. Brass elbow-jointed, sliding stays were fixed at the sides; or oak bearers, running in slots just below the level of the flap hinges, could be pulled out at each side, to act as cantilever supports. The front ends of these bearers were faced with walnut and fitted with small brass knob or loop handles. Drawers were generally oak-lined, and in the small drawers of the top some very minute work is to be found, the linings often being less than one eighth of an inch thick, but perfectly dovetailed. In such positions the oak has kept remarkably fresh-looking.[1]

Beside the well-made brass pulls and escutcheons, the large drawers, flaps and doors of cabinets, etc., were fitted with locks of excellent workmanship. At the foot of the upper stage candle-slides were usually fitted, consisting of thin oak trays, cross-framed at the ends and running in slots; they were faced with walnut

---

[1] The bureau in two stages of stock size measuring three feet six inches has two doors, the rare smaller size (which is two feet wide) has usually one door.

and had small brass pulls. Some walnut specimens are found with veneered door panels instead of mirrors, but in most cases they are a substitution for the original glass.

Bookcases with glazed doors made during the walnut period are extremely rare.

In the tall, glazed bookcase which lent itself to architectural treatment, doors were divided by stout bars into rectangular panes.

Bookcases were designed in two general types:

(1) With front composed of two glazed doors surmounted by a cornice, the interior fitted with shelves adjustable on side racks, the whole supported on a low stand.

(2) With the upper part mounted upon a broader and deeper base, fronted with low glazed doors, or containing deep drawers, and resting upon ball or bun turned feet or corner brackets.

These bookcases usually had an oak carcase dovetailed at the angles and veneered with walnut. The back was of panelled oak. The doors were faced with walnut cross-banding, the mouldings and the glazing bars being in cross-grain walnut. The glass panes were frequently bevelled.

There were three phases in the design of glazing bars. The first was of a simple rounded section (similar to the half-round mould around the drawers in contemporary chests) projecting above the surface-level of the doors, and glued down to a backing strip of oak, which it over-lapped on each side. It was generally formed in short, cross-grain lengths.

The second (contemporary with the first) had a square fillet added on each side, and dates from about 1675. It did not rise above the door surface, and was usually in solid work; this was followed in the early mahogany and very late walnut period by a third fillet added at the apex of the curve, forming the ovolo moulded bar.

It was usual to secure the glass with brads and putty.

Some cabinets were finely made in oak—probably by joiners rather than cabinet-makers—and polished without any veneered surface, in which cases it followed that the bar work was never in cross-grained wood. The finest of this type are the bookcases in the Pepysian Library, Magdalene College, Cambridge. It is very probable that reasons of construction induced the change to the bar with side and central fillets, this section having proved the strongest and most convenient in sticking—i.e., running the moulding by plane—and in mitring and tenoning at the passing joints in window work. A few cabinets are known designed with glazed panels at their sides, but are extremely rare.

Illustrations on pages 130-133.

X

CORNER CUPBOARDS

THE first printed reference to a corner cupboard appears in 1711.[1] Corner cupboards to stand or to hang in the angles of rooms were made in oak, walnut, mahogany or in japanned soft wood, and a large number of specimens exist. They were made either with a flat front and short returns to abut on the walls at right angles, or were bow-fronted. The standing cupboards were in one or two sections; in the latter case, both parts were fitted with doors, the upper one sometimes glazed to display the china and glass on the shelves.

Those designed as a small single cupboard with solid panelled door obtained a large amount of support on the dado moulding which was invariably fitted around rooms, and in addition nails or screws were driven through the back boards into the plaster or wall panelling. The greater number of corner cupboards can be assigned to the late eighteenth century.

The interiors were fitted with shelves having a shaped front edge, and often grooved close to the back edges to support plates; the back boards were generally painted a dull green on the inside. During the last quarter of the century both the oak and mahogany specimens were often inlaid with borders, and with small shells and paterae; and many were fitted with small drawers immediately beneath or inside the cupboard. The cornices were of similar type to those found on contemporary cabinets, and when on the bow front were built up of narrow sections to obviate end grain coming to the face near the sides. When flat-fronted, cupboards were sometimes pedimented, and in very rare cases in the bow front also.

Illustration on page 123.

[1] Advertisement of Isaac van den Helm, *Postman*, March 8-10, 1711. An earlier reference occurs in the Great Wardrobe Accounts for 1692.

XI

CHESTS OF DRAWERS

THE use of veneer upon the carcase of a chest of drawers revolutionized its appearance, and the panelled and mitred drawer fronts characteristic of the middle years of the seventeenth century disappeared; and the division into a number of deep drawers, surmounted by two shallow drawers became established.

Chests of drawers may be divided into three groups:

1 Those about three feet three inches high containing, as a rule, five drawers, a projecting large ovolo mould around the top edge or a small cornice, and a projecting plinth mould (the latter often being an inversion of the cornice), a short vertical plinth, largely cut away, leaving bracket feet at the corners, whose inner edges were shaped. Alternatively, beneath the plinth mould the supports consisted of large ball or bun-turned feet.

A common practice was the placing of the top drawer or drawers right up under the small cornice, and the bottom drawer tight down on the plinth mould, which is found worn at the sides where the drawer has rubbed.

2 The chest itself, though in cases possessing only four drawers, rests upon a low stand consisting of four, five, or six legs tied with stretchers. They can rarely be dated prior to William III's reign. The frieze of the stand which is similar in all details to contemporary side tables, frequently contained drawers.

3 The tallboy chest of drawers, dating from about 1710, which can be subdivided:

(a) A lower portion but with its top mould, projecting or not, always receding inwards as a plinth for the upper chest (which may have a small base mould in addition), and is less in width and depth than the under chest. The top chest frequently had three long drawers and a top row of three drawers.

99

(*b*) As (*a*) but the lower chest contained fewer drawers, due to its being mounted on cabriole legs; in fact, in some examples the lower part must be termed a stand with drawers.

Common characteristics of tallboys are the splayed corners, frequently found on the upper chest, though also found on the lower chest or the stand. They were wide chamfers faced with thin cross-grained pieces of walnut, finishing at their lower ends in a graceful curve by which the splay was 'stopped' and brought out to the right-angled corner. At the top the splay continued into the cornice, with which the mouldings (usually an ogee or cyma over a large cavetto) also complied. Vertical fluting or applied frets decorated the chamfer.

Many chests and cabinets were conceived almost as architectural compositions, their fine proportions and mouldings bringing them into line with the decorative woodwork of rooms. The carcase was of yellow deal in flat unpanelled surfaces about one inch thick, formed of boards glued together with the grain, the sides, top, and bottom being dovetailed together. The horizontal divisions between the drawers were housed into the sides and extended the full depth of the chest. The angle bracket feet beneath the plinth mould, while appearing to support the chest, did not always do so; the brackets were usually mitred at the angles, and in the internal angle was placed a square block coming directly under the corner of the body and taking the weight; and projecting a fraction of an inch below the brackets. Following a Dutch practice, the sides of chests, cabinets, and bureaux were sometimes left unveneered, but the better examples were overlaid with figured or straight-grain walnut, panel effects being obtained by laying a border strip of cross-banded veneer (the grain across the direction of the band) and by the narrow feather or herring-bone inlay an inch or two from the edge. The cornice and plinth moulds were always worked across the grain—i.e., on the splayed deal backing a row of short and often wedge-shaped pieces of solid walnut were glued closely together, and with the grain vertical for the whole length of the member, with mitred angles. When set, the moulding plane was run along to produce the required profile.

In some chests on stands and some tallboys the cornice was given an architectural character in the following ways:

(*a*) There was a top projecting moulding or cornice proper, beneath which was a swell or pulvinated frieze, both veneered in cross-grain walnut (the latter usually the front of a drawer). Beneath this frieze was a very narrow moulded necking or architrave strip.

EXAMPLES of CORNICE PROFILES; 17TH & 18TH C^{IES}

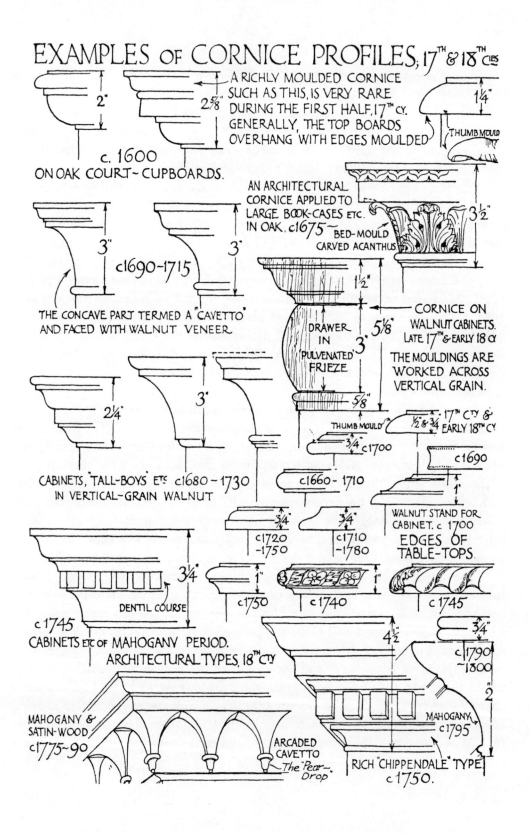

A RICHLY MOULDED CORNICE SUCH AS THIS, IS VERY RARE DURING THE FIRST HALF, 17TH CY. GENERALLY, THE TOP BOARDS OVERHANG WITH EDGES MOULDED

2"

2⅝"

c. 1600
ON OAK COURT~CUPBOARDS.

1¼"

THUMB MOULD

AN ARCHITECTURAL CORNICE APPLIED TO LARGE BOOK-CASES ETC. IN OAK. c1675

BED-MOULD CARVED ACANTHUS

3½"

3"

3"

c1690~1715

THE CONCAVE PART TERMED A "CAVETTO" AND FACED WITH WALNUT VENEER.

1½"

5⅝"

3"

DRAWER IN "PULVENATED" FRIEZE

5/8"

CORNICE ON WALNUT CABINETS. LATE 17TH & EARLY 18 C^Y

THE MOULDINGS ARE WORKED ACROSS VERTICAL GRAIN.

½ & ¾ 17TH CY & EARLY 18TH CY

2¼"

3"

THUMB MOULD

¾ c1700

c1660~1710

c1690

1"

CABINETS, "TALL-BOYS" E^{TS} c1680~1730 IN VERTICAL~GRAIN WALNUT.

WALNUT STAND FOR CABINET. c 1700

EDGES OF TABLE-TOPS.

¾
c1720 ~1750

¾
c1710 ~1780

1" c1750

1" c1740

c1745

3¼"

DENTIL COURSE

c 1745
CABINETS ETC OF MAHOGANY PERIOD.
ARCHITECTURAL TYPES, 18TH C^{TY}

¾
c1790 ~1800

4½"

2"

MAHOGANY & SATIN-WOOD c1775~90

ARCADED CAVETTO ~The "Pear~ Drop"

RICH "CHIPPENDALE" TYPE c1750.

MAHOGANY c1795

(*b*) The cornice, largely composed of a cavetto (with smaller members above and below) was arched, either centrally with a continuation of straight cornice on each side, or there was a double (and rarely a treble) arching of almost complete semicircles. The cavetto was overlaid with vertical veneer and the small mouldings on cross-grain facing strips. Turned finials were often added at the corners and above the level of the mitred junctions of the arches.

(*c*) The cornice was formed as a pediment, pointed or curved (generally the latter), and of large cavetto section. It was formed in 'broken' fashion (with the centre part omitted) and the gap was filled by a small stand or pedestal for a vase or turned finial. This type is very rare on tallboys, and was not adopted until about the second decade of the eighteenth century. The mouldings or beads around the front of drawers varied considerably. The earliest found on walnut pieces, which is a half round applied beading fixed to the carcase and surrounding the drawer, dates during the reign of William and Mary. Succeeding this is the double half round bead, fixed to the carcase, and dating during the first fifteen years of the eighteenth century. The cock (or cocked) bead which followed, a small moulding applied to the edges of drawer fronts, was introduced about 1730, and continued to be used throughout the century.

In various pieces of country origin, made in solid oak throughout, borders of cross-banded walnut were often let in on the solid drawer fronts. The faces of the drawer fronts were veneered with vertical grain walnut or oyster wood; the positions of escutcheon and handle plates were chosen to place the vertical joins in the veneer, the lines of the figure or grain being opposed about these points with added effect; the borders were generally cross-banded and feathered, used either together or singly. Occasionally on examples dating from about 1730, a little strip inlay of geometrical pattern in holly and ebony was used; but this is unusual and frequently has been added subsequently or denotes Dutch work.

The drawers were of oak or deal, according to the quality of the piece; often the veneered front was deal, while the sides, back, and bottom were oak; the common dovetail, at first used at all four angles, presented too much end grain where the veneered border was laid on the face; consequently, lap dovetailing was substituted. The top edges of the sides were usually rounded, the lower edges were either rebated or left square, and the boards of the bottom were nailed up into them; the latter were fixed with grain going from front to back. In the walnut chests dating from the reign of George I the drawer sides were grooved to provide a housing for the bottom boards. Some chests, dating from about 1680, had their tops (if of low type), their drawer fronts, and sometimes their sides also, inlaid with panels and borders of marquetry. When this was employed the ground was usually of straight-grained walnut, or of oyster wood. Small chests with a hinged folding top are termed to-day 'bachelor chests', but there appears to be no early evidence of the use of this term.

Illustrations on pages 134-136.

XII

DRESSERS

DRESSERS, which appear to have developed into the well-known form in the seventeenth century, were similar to long side tables, with the addition of drawers and cupboards beneath the top. They exhibit the characteristics in mouldings and enrichment of contemporary work and many examples exist dating from the second half of the seventeenth century. In dressers of table form the front legs are of varied baluster form, the back legs being flat posts. During the walnut period oak dressers were in some cases enriched with cross-banded borders in walnut round drawer edges. During the eighteenth century a few were made in mahogany, but oak was always the prevailing wood. There are also late eighteenth century examples of oak banded with mahogany.

Having a constant function the dresser changed but little, except to add a superstructure with shelves and small cupboards during the eighteenth century. To their original owners, farmers and yeomen, fashion was of little consequence. The cabriole leg, which appears on dressers in the second part of the eighteenth century, remained a long time in use; and a cornice or curtain was sometimes added to topmost tier of shelves. A pierced apron, which is often found in Welsh dressers, is a decorative feature, and there is a tendency to provide a large number of drawers and cupboards during the late eighteenth century.

Illustrations on page 64.

XIII

BEDS

BEDROOMS were placed among the principal rooms on the first floor, and it was customary to hold receptions therein. In these rooms the height of the interiors was considerable. This affected the treatment of the bed, which, after the Restoration, became the field for the display of textiles, feathers and fringes. Survivals of this period are rare, but the Royal Wardrobe accounts give particulars of richly upholstered beds supplied for the Royal Palaces during the reign of Charles II and that of James II. An example dating from late in Charles II's reign (formerly at Glemham in Suffolk) is hung with crimson velvet and the cornice, curtains and valance are trimmed with silk fringe. Already under the last two Stuart kings, the cornice was covered with a textile and fringed. Under William III there was a further increase in the invasion of upholstery, and the cornice, head-board and tester were carved in white wood over which was pasted damask or velvet outlined with braid or fringe. The projection of the broken and voluted scrolls, cartouches and other ornaments was in considerable relief; and the cornice was sometimes pierced. The posts, also covered, were hidden by the curtains. During the first quarter of the eighteenth century beds were drawn upwards in keeping with the great height of rooms, and there is no longer any attempt to simulate in textiles the folds and loopings of drapery. The design tends to elaborate architectural forms and mouldings, and the great height of the bed is sometimes emphasized by engaged columns carried up the headboard to the tester.

Damask seems to have been preferred as a covering in the tall beds dating from the early years of the eighteenth century, such as the bed covered with rose-coloured damask at Hampton Court Palace, made for George, Prince of Wales, in 1715.

A half-tester bed (the French *lit d'ange*) also appears in the Royal accounts of the late seventeenth century. In this type there were no posts, and the tester is reduced in size. These Royal beds, which were covered with velvets and damasks, were usually made by French upholsterers whose names are entered in the Royal Wardrobe accounts. Beds of the late seventeenth century and early eighteenth century of modest size and simple design exist, such as the example from Boughton House[1] where the wood work is covered with moiré enriched with applied work.

Illustration on page 137.

[1] In the Victoria and Albert Museum (1067-1916) which is fourteen feet high.

XIV

MIRRORS AND DRESSING GLASSES

THE art of making mirror plates was an imported one in England, and their supply in quantity dates from the establishment of a factory at Vauxhall by the Duke of Buckingham shortly after the Restoration. This manufacture was carried on 'with amazing success' until the late eighteenth century, though in the early years of the eighteenth century it was rivalled by the glass house at the Bear garden in Southwark.

The property of reflection was obtained by the use of tinfoil coated thinly with mercury, upon which the glass was laid and subjected to pressure to obtain adhesion. This process would necessarily restrict the size of the mirror; and early Vauxhall plates were limited to a length of about forty-five inches. The thickness of Vauxhall plate was little more than half that of the modern glass, and the bevel at the edges was so flat as to be almost imperceptible. These mirrors were first mounted in rectangular frames made of deal, of flattish convex section, and three and a half to five and a half inches in width. The frame was veneered in cross-banded or oyster walnut and on fine examples marquetry was inlaid in continuous designs or in reserves. Sections of ebony veneer and tortoiseshell were also used as enrichments for frames.

These mirrors also served for the dressing mirrors until the swinging mirror was introduced in Anne's reign. Above the broad moulded frames a fret-cut and pierced cresting was invariably fixed, but many of these have been lost. This type of mirror was of square proportions, and was in use throughout the reign of William III. Early in the eighteenth century the proportion changed to a narrow and tall shape, with narrow, flat, cross-banded frame, shaped at the top and with fret-cut cresting. These mirrors were hung in the piers between the windows, and it was customary to place a side table beneath them. During the early eighteenth century, the value of gilt or parcel-gilt framing of the mirror was recognized, and frames were decorated in gilt gesso. In these, the appearance of height was usually emphasized by the narrowness of the sides of the frame, which contrasted with the base and cresting.

Another type of mirror frame was narrow, and of simple rounded section in cross-grain walnut, shaped at the top with S or ogee curves and arch forms, to all of which the glass was shaped and bevelled. All these mirror frames were invariably of deal construction, either lap-halved or mitred at the corners, and on the many curved parts laminated for necessary strength.

In one type there is an outer frame worked with a fretted outline, and the top enclosed a carved and gilt shell or medallion.

The mirror plates were often cut into patterns on portions of the face. In rare cases small paintings are found on the back of the glass where it is left unsilvered. On tall mirrors the plate was usually in two pieces. There was no attempt to hide the junction, at which both plates were often bevelled. Another usual position for the mirror was immediately above the chimney piece. The chimney glass, extending the width of the chimney piece and resting on it, was divided into three sections, of which the junction was marked by applied strips of glass. There are many examples of chimney mirrors of this type at Hampton Court Palace, dating from the reign of William III.

The dressing glass, an introduction of the early eighteenth century, was usually similar to the narrow-framed wall mirrors, and on some there is a fret-cut cresting. Frequently a gilt fillet bordered the bevelled plate. Such glasses were attached by screw-action mirror movements to a pair of plainly turned or straight, fluted, slender uprights (slightly raking backwards), which at their bases were framed into a small box constructed of deal, veneered in walnut, and fitted with several small drawers in one, two, or three tiers, which receded towards the upper tier and were often shaped in front. The drawers were oak-lined in very thin work, the fronts veneered, and fitted with brass pulls. The small feet varied, but were usually of the corner bracket type. On some examples the set of drawers was enclosed with a slanting flap and had draw-out side bearers like a miniature bureau; in others the sides were sloped as if to receive the flap, but the front is left open.

Another type had the mirror mounted on a bureau with slant flap (about two feet wide); beneath, two long drawers were generally fitted, and the whole was carried on slender cabriole legs.

Illustrations on pages 138-142.

XV

LONG-CASE CLOCK CASES

THE form of the long-case ('grandfather') clock was conditioned by the requirements of clockwork, and followed the use of the anchor escapement which permitted the long pendulum to be used in a contracted space. The tall wooden case supported the movement and the dial at a convenient height, and also protected the weights from interference. The pendulum clock came in at the Restoration of Monarchy and an important school of clock-making developed from this period.

There are three parts to the case: at the top the hood, covering the dial and mechanism; below this the body, enclosing the weights and pendulum; and the base, utilized also as a space for weight travel. The clocks of the age of walnut are slender and graceful in their proportions. During the Restoration period the height of the long-case clock was six feet, but increased in height to nine feet or more in the early eighteenth century. The carcase was of oak; in fine cases this was veneered, usually with walnut, and sometimes with ebony, olivewood, kingwood and laburnum. Parquetry of figured woods and marquetry were employed during the late seventeenth and early eighteenth centuries. From the earliest examples until about 1720 the cornice of the hood was usually straight and flat-topped, and occasionally crowned with a shaped and carved pediment. Spiral columns were usually placed at the angles until about 1700, but the plain turned shaft with caps and bases moulded in brass had come in about a decade earlier.

Frets, which were used to provide an outlet for the sound of the bell, were applied to the frieze of the hood after about 1675. The glazed hood door was square, cross-banded on the frame, or inlaid with marquetry.

The hood was broader and deeper than the body, which necessitated an important moulding at their junction, and upon the top member of this the angle columns stood (the front pair being rebated on to the sides of the hood door). This moulding should be compared with that by which the body spreads out at the base. Invariably, up to about 1705, they will be found to differ, but after that

THE LONG CASE CLOCK.

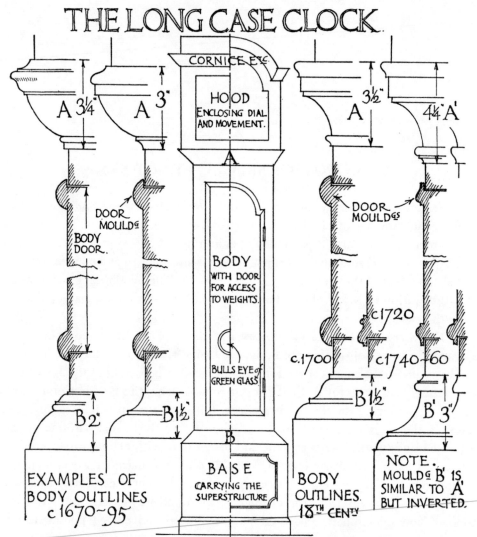

A 3¼"

A 3"

CORNICE ETC.

HOOD
ENCLOSING DIAL
AND MOVEMENT.

A 3½"

4¼ A'

DOOR
MOULDᵍ

DOOR
MOULDᵍˢ

BODY
DOOR.

A

c1720

c.1700

c.1740-60

BODY
WITH DOOR
FOR ACCESS
TO WEIGHTS.

BULLS EYE of
GREEN GLASS

B 2"

B 1½"

B 1½"

B' 3"

B

EXAMPLES OF
BODY OUTLINES
c 1670~95

BASE
CARRYING THE
SUPERSTRUCTURE

BODY
OUTLINES.
18ᵀᴴ CENᵀʸ

NOTE.
MOULDᵍ B' IS
SIMILAR TO A'
BUT INVERTED.

COMPARATIVE FEATURES.

FROM c1670 UNTIL c 1720

FROM c1740 UNTIL c 1760

FROM c1670 UNTIL c 1720	FROM c1740 UNTIL c 1760
CORNICE STRAIGHT; DOMED c1695~1705	CORNICE USUALLY ARCHED, NO DOME,
HOOD DOOR SQUARE HEADED.	OFTEN A FRET CUT CRESTING & FINIALS.
BODY DOOR, SQUARE HEADED.	HOOD & BODY DOORS ARCHED.
GLASS BULLS-EYE IN CASE DOOR	MOULD A SIMILAR TO B, AFTER c1710.
MOULDᵍ A, DISSIMILAR FROM B	COLUMNS AT ANGLES OF HOOD, TURNED
COLUMNS AT ANGLES OF HOOD, USUALLY	DORIC OR CORINTHIAN, BRASS CAPS &
TWIST TURNED, c1670~ c1705	BASES: CASE VENEERED MAHOGANY, &
CASE VENEERED WALNUT; MANY IN	IN LACQUER. BRASS & PAINTED IRON DIALS.
MARQUETERIE, ALSO RED, BLACK, AND	VERY FEW LONG CASE CLOCKS MADE IN
GREEN LACQUER. BRASS DIALS	EARLY YEARS OF MAHOGANY PERIOD.

approximate date the trend of design was to utilize the same mould, a large cavetto, in both positions. The front of the body consisted almost entirely of the door, which was square-headed until about 1720. A little below half its height an oval or circular hole was pierced, and glazed with a glass 'bull's-eye', generally of a greenish hue, enclosed in a brass frame. The door had a small half-round mould of cross-grain walnut fixed around and projecting over its edge and covering the joint with the body frame. The door and the base front were both treated as panels.

Clock cases were also made with a hood of flattened dome form, surmounted by brass or turned gilt finials set at the two front corners and centrally on the dome. They were rare prior to 1700.

There was a slight variation in the short plinths. The majority were solid, but some examples had a shaped base line with angle brackets.

Seaweed and endive marquetry was used on fine clock cases in the first years of the eighteenth century. Early in George I's reign marquetry was outmoded, and cases were either of walnut veneer or decorated by japanning. During the first decade of the eighteenth century the increased height of the case was accompanied by the arching of the hood.

Illustrations on page 143.

XVI

STANDS FOR LIGHTS

AMONG the innovations of the early Restoration period was the portable stand for a candlestick.[1] In notices of sales in journals and in inventories of household furniture, 'a pair of stands' is frequently listed in connection with a table; and some complete sets of table and stands have survived. The stand consists of a top, a shaft, and a three-centred base, which had the advantage of stability and of finding a level upon an uneven floor. 'A little round table set upon one pillar or poste' was used according to the *Academy of Armory* (1688) 'both as a bason stand, and to support a candle to read by'. The form of the shaft in the late seventeenth century was a plain or spiral baluster, directly supporting a small circular or polygonal tray top. Early in the reign of George I, a set of gilt candle-stands made at Hampton Court Palace have a vase-shaped member immediately beneath the top, a square shaft and tripod base of double scroll form.

Illustrations on page 144.

[1] An oak example dating from about 1640 is illustrated in the *Dictionary of English Furniture*, Vol. III, p. 141.

53. VENEER of walnut oyster pieces, enriched with floral marquetry in reserves. Table top. *c.* 1685.

54. CUPBOARD, of oak, decorated with inlay of mother-of-pearl and bone in reserves. *c.* 1660. From Baddesley Clinton, Warwickshire.

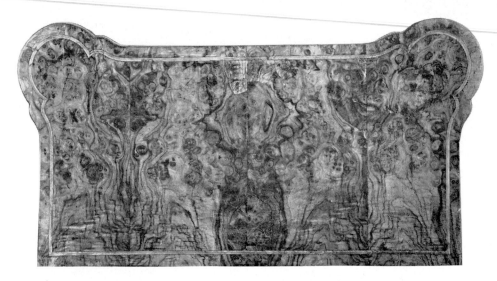

55. BURR WALNUT VENEER (from a table top). Early eighteenth century.

56. PARQUETRY OF KINGWOOD.

57. DETAIL OF BASE OF A JAPANNED CLOCK by James Markwick. *c.* 1720. From the Victoria and Albert Museum.

58. BUREAU CABINET, the exterior japanned in gold on a black ground, (the desk fitting of mahogany). Mid-eighteenth century. From Mr. Leonard Knight.

Height, 8 ft
Width, 4 ft

59. SINGLE CHAIR, of oak, with spiral uprights and stretchers and slat back, painted with a small floral pattern on a black ground. *c.* 1660. From the Duke of Devonshire, Hardwick Hall, Derbyshire.

60. ARMCHAIR, of oak, the framework composed of knob-turnings. *c.* 1650–1660. From Doddington Hall, Lincolnshire.

61. DOUBLE CHAIR, the framework enriched with S-scrolls and spiral turning. From St. Martin's Church, Ludgate Hill. Dated 1690, and bearing initials of two church-wardens.

62. ARMCHAIR, the framework enriched with spiral carving and acanthus scrolls. *c.* 1680. From the Earl of Sandwich, Hichingbrooke, Huntingdonshire.

Height, 4 ft   *Width*, 2 ft 1¼ ins

63. ARMCHAIR, the back finely carved in the French taste, the legs connected by a moulded cross stretcher. *c.* 1695. From Brigadier W. Clark.

> *Height*, 4 ft 4 ins
> *Width*, 2 ft 2 $\frac{1}{2}$ ins

64. ARMCHAIR, with narrow back panel bordered with pierced scroll work, and spiral uprights, dated 1699. The scroll-shaped legs and arm-supports are pierced. The cresting is carved with the arms of Cann of Bristol. From Mr. F. Partridge.

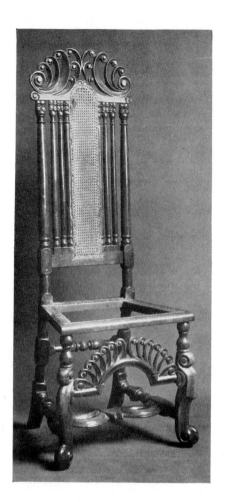

65. SINGLE CHAIR, with back formed of balusters on either side of a narrow caned panel, surmounted by a cresting of short scrolls. *c*. 1690. From Woolbeding Rectory, Sussex.

66. MASTER'S CHAIR, the cresting carved with the arms of the Parish Clerk's Company, the back and seat caned. *c*. 1690. (Given to the Company in 1716.)

Height, 5 ft ½ in

68. ARMCHAIR, the cabriole legs united by stretchers, the covering (much worn) of silk. Early eighteenth century. From the Duke of Buccleuch, Boughton, Northamptonshire.

Height, 3 ft 6½ ins   *Width,* 2 ft 4 ins

9. SINGLE CHAIR with lion paw feet, the legs
arved with a lion's mask. *c.* 1735. From Brigadier
V. Clark.

Height, 3 ft 5 ins   *Width*, 2 ft 1½ ins

70. SINGLE CHAIR (one of a set), with splat veneered
with straight-grained walnut, and legs hipped on to
the seat-rail. Early eighteenth century. From Baddesley Clinton, Warwickshire.

Single chairs

71. CHAIR, with upholstered seat and back, the carved legs hipped on to the seat rail. *c.* 1715. From Sir John Carew Pole, Bart., Antony House, Cornwall.

Height, 3 ft 1 in
Width, 1 ft 10½ ins

72. CHAIR, with pierced splat and shaped and carved top rail. *c.* 1715. From the Earl of Sandwich, Hinchingbrooke, Huntingdonshire.

Height, 3 ft 3 ins
Width, 2 ft 1 in

73. WRITING CHAIR,
the splat inlaid with
the crest of Legh. *c.*
1725. From Lyme Park,
Cheshire.

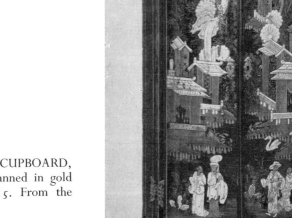

74. HANGING CORNER CUPBOARD,
surmounted by shelves; japanned in gold
on a black ground. *c.* 1715. From the
Edward Hudson Collection.

   Height, 4 ft
   Length, 1 ft 11½ ins
   Depth, 1 ft 4 ins

75. LONG STOOL, the seat rail shaped, and the legs connected by a stretcher. *c.* 1710. From Erthig, Denbighshire.

Height, 1 ft 4 ins   *Length,* 3 ft $7\frac{5}{8}$ ins

76. STOOL, with caned seat and scroll-shaped legs connected by a cross stretcher. *c.* 1660–70. From Hall Place, Bexley, Kent.

77. LONG STOOL, the seat covered with cut velvet (early eighteenth century), the legs connected by a rising stretcher. *c.* 1690. From Hampton Court Palace, Middlesex.

78. STOOL, the baluster-shaped legs finishing in scroll feet, and united by a moulded cross-stretcher (the velvet of the early eighteenth century). *c.* 1690. From Hampton Court Palace, Middlesex.

Height, 1 ft 6 ins   *Length*, 2 ft 2 ins

79. SETTEE, the wide splat formed of vertical slats, the legs finishing in claw and ball feet. *c.* 1730. From Lord Doverdale, Westwood Park, Worcestershire.

Height, 3 ft 1½ ins   *Width,* 5 ft

80. SETTEE, the back and seat rail veneered with richly figured walnut, the arms finishing in birds' heads, the legs in claw and ball feet. From Chetham's Hospital, Manchester.

Height, 3 ft 7 ins   *Width,* 5 ft ½ in

81. SETTEE, the back and seat covered with turkey work. Early eighteenth century. From Cotehele, Cornwall.

Height, 3 ft 4 ins   *Length*, 4 ft 8 ins

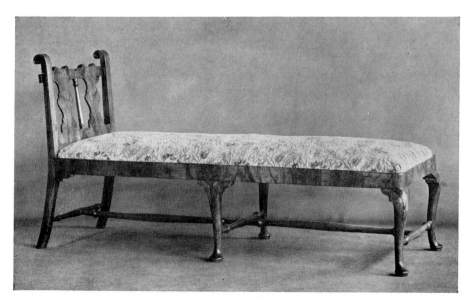

82. DAY-BED, with adjustable headrest. Early eighteenth century. From the Victoria and Albert Museum.

Height, 2 ft 9¾ ins   *Length*, 5 ft 8 ins

83. SIDE TABLE, with parqueted top, the legs inlaid with cross-banding. *c.* 1715. From Mrs. David Gubbay's Collection.

84. GATE-LEG TABLE of yew inlaid with sycamore. Late seventeenth century. From the Victoria and Albert Museum.

Height, 2 ft 4¼ ins   *Length* (flaps extended), 4 ft 11 ins

85. TABLE, with tray top. Early eighteenth century. From the James
Montagu Collection, Cold Overton Hall, Leicestershire.

Height, 2 ft *Length*, 2 ft 4 ins

86. CARD TABLE, the frieze and top parqueted with
olive wood and laburnum. *c.* 1715. From the Victoria
and Albert Museum. *Height* (open), 2 ft 4 ins

87. BUREAU, of mahogany, veneered with walnut and yew, the interior of the desk screened with amboyna. *c.* 1710. From the Victoria and Albert Museum.

Height, 3 ft 5 ins
Width, 3 ft

88. BUREAU, of knee-hole form; the top folds back and the flap (when closed) is flush with the top. *c.* 1700. From the Duke of Buccleuch, Boughton, Northampton-shire.

Height, 3 ft 2½ ins
Width, 3 ft 7 ins

89. BUREAU, veneered with straight grained walnut. Early eighteenth century. From Hotspur, Richmond.

90. WRITING TABLE, the hinged top supported on ratchets. The pilasters and top drawer draw out to support the flap when horizontal. From Hotspur, Richmond.

91. KNEE-HOLE WRITING TABLE, veneered with kingwood. From Hotspur, Richmond.

92. WRITING TABLE, supported on cabriole legs. Early eighteenth century. From the Duke of Buccleuch, Boughton, Northamptonshire.

Height, 3 ft 6 ins   *Width*, 4 ft 7 ins

93. BUREAU CABINET, veneered with stained burr elm, the cross-bandings bordered by pewter stringing lines. (Probably by Coxed and Woster.) *c.* 1690. From Crooksbury, Surrey.

    Height, 7 ft   *Width,* 3 ft 5 ins

94. CHEST OF DRAWERS, on stand with spiral turned supports. *c.* 1680. From the G. L. Riley Collection.

> *Height*, 4 ft 11 ins
> *Width*, 3 ft 2½ ins

95. CHEST OF DRAWERS, on stand, the baluster-shaped feet connected by a shaped stretcher. *c.* 1690. From Lytes Cary, Somerset.

> *Height*, 5 ft 9 ins
> *Width*, 3 ft 6½ ins

96. CHEST OF DRAWERS, on stand. *c.* 1715. From the
Victoria and Albert Museum.
> *Height*, 5 ft 8⅞ ins
> *Width*, 3 ft 4¾ ins

97. CHEST OF DRAWERS, on stand (the
knob handles of the drawer of the stand
modern). *c.* 1680. From Baddesley Clinton,
Warwickshire.

Tallboy (double chest of drawers)

98. DOUBLE CHEST OF DRAWERS (tallboy), the angles of the upper stage faced with pilasters. *c.* 1720. From Phillips of Hitchin, Hertfordshire.

Height, 6 ft 6 ins   *Width,* 3 ft 7¾ ins

99. BED, hung with crimson velvet trimmed with silver galon. (Made for William III.)
c. 1690. From Hampton Court Palace, Middlesex.

   Height (to top of plumes), 17 ft

100. MIRROR, in convex
frame inlaid with reserves of
floral marquetry. Late seventeenth century. From the College, Kirkoswald, Yorkshire.
    Height, 2 ft 11$\frac{3}{4}$ ins
    Width, 2 ft 7 ins

101. MIRROR, in convex frame enriched
with bandings, the cresting bordered with
fretwork. *c.* 1690. From Lord Leconfield,
Petworth, Sussex.

102. MIRROR, in narrow gilt frame,
carved in reserves. Early eighteenth
century. From Sir John Carew Pole,
Bart., Antony House, Cornwall.

Height, 2 ft 3 ins
Width, 1 ft 7½ ins

103. MIRROR, in narrow frame, with shaped
cresting and apron. *c.* 1720. From the G. L. Riley
Collection.

Height, 4 ft 6 ins

104. MIRROR, in a narrow gilt frame, the cresting and apron carved in gesso, with details in carved wood. *c.* 1725.

105. MIRROR, veneered with walnut enriched with carved and gilt mouldings and details. *c.* 1730. From the Bank House, Wisbech.

106. DRESSING GLASS, showing interior fittings of stand. *c.* 1710. From the G. L. Riley Collection.

Height, 3 ft 1 in

107. DRESSING GLASS, japanned in gold on a red ground, the drawer fitted for toilet requisites, the desk portion with small drawers and pigeon-holes. *c.* 1715.

Height, 3 ft 4 ins
Width, 1 ft 6 ins

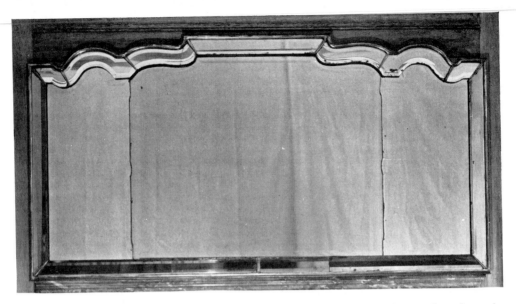

108. CHIMNEY GLASS, of three plates, framed in a moulded glass border. Early eighteenth century.

109. CHIMNEY GLASS in raised, carved and gilt frame, the upper portion containing a sea-scape by Peter Monamy. *c.* 1740. From the Victoria and Albert Museum.

Height, 3 ft 10 ins   *Width*, 5 ft 7 ins

110. LONG-CASE CLOCK, veneered with walnut enriched with floral marquetry. (The movement by William Speakman.) A gift to the Vintners' Company in 1704. From the Vintners' Company.

Height, 8 ft 9 ins

111. LONG-CASE CLOCK, veneered with burr walnut, the stepped and domed hood surmounted by finials. (The movement by Thomas Tompion.) *c.* 1700. From the Tallow Chandlers' Company.

Height, 9 ft 6 ins

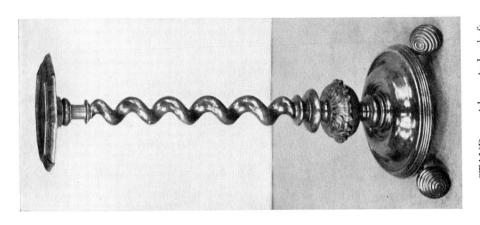

114. STAND, with spiral shaft. Late seventeenth century. From Mr. Leonard Knight.

Height, 3 ft 3 ins

113. TRIPOD TABLE, with scalloped tray top. First quarter of eighteenth century. From Sir John Ramsden's Collection, Bulstrode Park, Buckinghamshire.

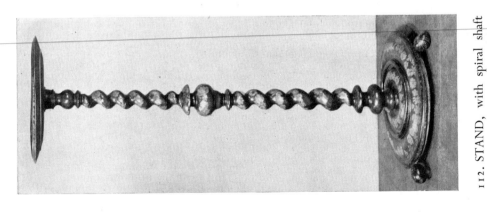

112. STAND, with spiral shaft painted with flowers on a blue-green ground. *c.* 1670. From Lyme Park, Cheshire. *Height*, 4 ft

PART THREE

THE PERIOD OF MAHOGANY, SATIN-WOOD AND ROSEWOOD FURNITURE

Circa 1720–1810

I

HISTORICAL NOTE

THE reign of George I is notable for the beginning of the invasion by the architect of the province of furniture design. In case-furniture, the proportions were based upon the classical orders, and the sections of moulding were copied. The architect William Kent (1684-1748) is also known as a designer of furniture. Accustomed by his early training in Italy to the baroque and monumental furniture of Italian palaces, surviving examples of his work designed for a few great houses are usually gilt or parcel-gilt. Kent's influence extended to 'all who were emulous for distinction by an ostentatious display of their consequence and wealth' and for these clients he 'changed the fashion of their chairs and tables'.[1] Other architects such as Henry Flitcroft[2] and John Vardy, also designed 'architects' furniture. This architectural bias can be dated from about 1720 to 1740 and had little effect upon the course of traditional design.

Architects' furniture can be recognized by its inability to suggest wood as the basis of its design, and by the embodiment (in case-furniture) of elements of classic architecture, such as columns, pilasters, and entablatures. This style went out of fashion by 1740, and was replaced by a version of the lively and pliant French *rocaille*, which became the 'epidemical distemper of the kingdom'. The *rocaille* had been practised by a number of brilliant French designers, such as François Cuvilliès, Juste-Aurèle Meissonnier, Gilles-Marie Oppenordt; its pioneer in this country was Matthias Lock, a lively draughtsman and carver of great ability, whose early designs antedate Chippendale's *Director* (1754) by a decade. His importance was first recognized by Fiske Kimball, in his *Creators of the*

[1] Pyne, *Royal Residences* (1819) Vol. 2.
[2] A side table (W-6, 1933) preserved in the Victoria and Albert Museum is by Flitcroft.

Chippendale Style (1929). In consequence, the importance of Thomas Chippendale as an innovator was much diminished. The *Director*, however, is interesting as illustrating not only the rococo, but the sub-styles, the Chinese and revived Gothic, which were sometimes oddly combined with it. There is little relevance in the choice of these 'tastes', or in their simultaneous presentation.

The Chinese taste, which appeared before the middle years of the eighteenth century, was a symptom of revolt against the Palladian tradition in decoration. Certain structural features of Chinese furniture were adopted, such as the outward curve of arms of armchairs, and details such as frets and card-cut lattice (or low relief lattice work on a solid ground) and the pagoda-shaped cresting were introduced. In mirror frames and chimney pieces, Chinese figures, dragons and exotic birds added their note of oriental fantasy. The taste which was decried by leading contemporary architects, but sponsored by carpenter architects (such as the Halfpennys) continued in fashion until the effective influence of the classical revival after 1765. The revived Gothic also had its advocates, many of whom were members of a 'little clan' of neo-romantics. The revival was sufficiently recognized as early as 1742 when Batty Langley issued his *Gothic Architecture Restored and Improved;* and Horace Walpole's additions to Strawberry Hill were projected in 1750. In furniture design, current models were 'improved' by Gothic details such as cusping and arcading, and a Decorated or Perpendicular window lent itself to reproduction on the doors of cabinets and bookcases. There is abundant evidence throughout this period of the ascendancy of French taste in the descriptive terms used for certain forms such as commodes *bergères* (anglicised as *barjairs*), *confidentes* and *duchesses*.

The widest influence during the classical revival of George III's reign was that of the architect Robert Adam, which made itself felt after his return from the continent in 1759. This revival first found expression in a few great houses in which furniture was an essential part of a consistent scheme. In giving consideration to decoration and furniture, Robert Adam was undertaking no more than was required of an eighteenth-century architect. In all important commissions the construction of the actual building, the shell which would house the decorations and furniture, was regarded as the first part of a comprehensive scheme. The furniture designed by Adam for his clients was part of a considered arrangement for rooms devised for the conduct of an elaborate social parade. When removed from their original setting, the connection between the furniture and the interiors is lost. As Adam writes, his designs for furniture were 'first invented for particular persons', but were later brought into general use, and the publication of his

DETAILS of VENEERED DRAWER FRONTS.

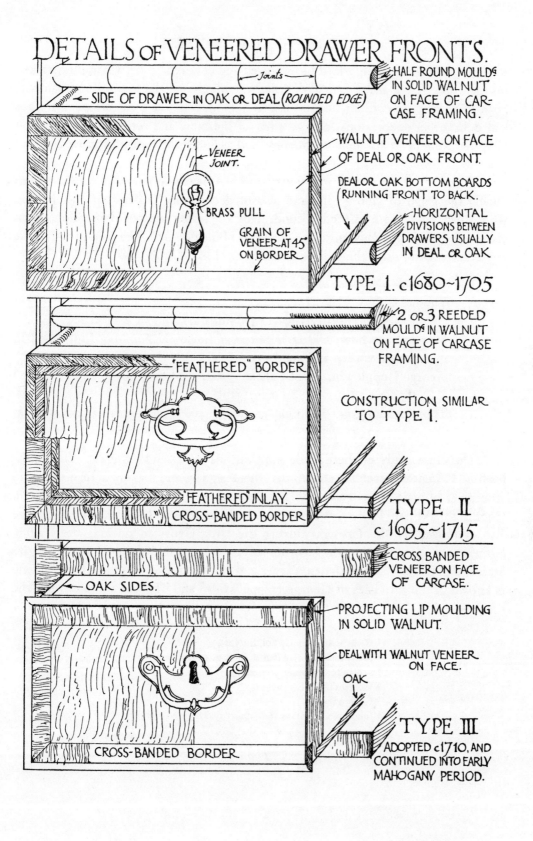

Joints

HALF ROUND MOULD⁵
IN SOLID WALNUT
ON FACE OF CAR-
CASE FRAMING.

← SIDE OF DRAWER IN OAK OR DEAL *(ROUNDED EDGE)*

VENEER
JOINT.

BRASS PULL

GRAIN OF
VENEER AT 45°
ON BORDER

WALNUT VENEER ON FACE
OF DEAL OR OAK FRONT.

DEAL OR OAK BOTTOM BOARDS
RUNNING FRONT TO BACK.

HORIZONTAL
DIVISIONS BETWEEN
DRAWERS USUALLY
IN DEAL OR OAK

TYPE 1. c 1680~1705

2 OR 3 REEDED
MOULD⁵ IN WALNUT
ON FACE OF CARCASE
FRAMING.

"FEATHERED" BORDER

CONSTRUCTION SIMILAR
TO TYPE 1.

'FEATHERED' INLAY.
CROSS-BANDED BORDER

TYPE II
c 1695~1715

CROSS BANDED
VENEER ON FACE
OF CARCASE.

← OAK SIDES.

PROJECTING LIP MOULDING
IN SOLID WALNUT.

DEAL WITH WALNUT VENEER
ON FACE.

OAK

TYPE III
ADOPTED c 1710, AND
CONTINUED INTO EARLY
MAHOGANY PERIOD.

CROSS-BANDED BORDER

Works in Architecture popularized his matured and coherent style. Characteristics of his furniture design are the small delicate mouldings and the low relief ornament, both in carving or composition. What he introduced was a calculated intricacy and delicacy in decoration, 'a new spirit of lightness and sensuous elegance, an elegance spidery in its delicate fineness and refined until all plastic feeling had gone'.[1]

There was a revival of marquetry and the use of veneers of exotic woods during the reign of George III, and also of decoration by painting either upon woodwork, or upon a painted ground. This vogue for painted decoration began about 1770, and continued until the last years of the century. The second half of the eighteenth century saw the publication of several trade catalogues.[2]

The best known of these are:

Thomas Chippendale, *The Gentleman's and Cabinet-makers' Director*, 1754, 1755 (2nd Edition) 1762 (3rd Edition).

Ince and Mayhew, *Universal System of Household Furniture* (published in parts between 1759 and 1763).

George Hepplewhite, *The Cabinet-makers' and Upholsterers' Guide* (1788) (Second edition, 1789, third edition 1794).

Thomas Sheraton, *The Cabinet-makers' and Upholsterers' Drawing Book*, 1791-1794.

The close study of these trade publications has been to a great extent misleading. Recent research has shown that the designers and makers of furniture who emerge as of major importance during the middle Georgian period are Benjamin Goodison,[3] William Hallett,[4] the partners William Vile and John Cobb, who were also employed by the Crown. During the later Georgian period, the leading figures were George Seddon,[5] owner of a 'great establishment' in Aldergate Street, and the brilliant designer, carver and cabinet-maker, John Linnell.[6] Little is known of the activities of George Heppelwhite[7] and Thomas Sheraton, but the *Guide* issued by the former in 1788 is a useful summary of the style of 1780-1785.

---

[1] *Works in Architecture*, Vol. II (No. 4).

[2] John Steegman, *The Rule of Taste*, p. 127.

[3] Benjamin Goodison, *fl. circa* 1727-1767.

[4] William Hallett, 1707-1781.

[5] George Seddon, 1727-1801.

[6] John Linnell, carver and cabinet-maker, died 1796.

[7] George Heppelwhite (died 1786).

HISTORICAL NOTE

Thomas Sheraton[1] was a designer rather than a maker of furniture, although he had been in early years a journeyman cabinet-maker. His importance lies in the quality of his designs which in his *Cabinet-makers' and Upholsterers' Drawing Book* cover the period between 1791 and 1794. His trade-card gives the information that he made designs for cabinet-makers, and from the text of the *Drawing Book* it is clear that he visited furniture makers to obtain information and assistance and to 'exhibit the present taste of furniture'.[2]

The influence of the French *Directoire* is in the ascendant during the last decade of the eighteenth century, when taste had reached the extreme limit of fastidious austerity. During this period the straight line is preferred in vertical and structural members, and it was pointed out by a critic that in ancient furniture[3] periods of cultivated taste were almost universally distinguished by straight and angular lines.

A feature of the late years of the century is the multiplication of types, and the creation of pieces for specialized use. By the evidence of pattern books and of surviving furniture there was a large variety of furniture to add to the comfort and convenience of life, especially for the dining room and the library.

The term Regency has been lately used to describe the English version of the classic style which was a lively offshoot of the French 'Empire'. During this new classical revival, a close reproduction of ancient furniture such as couches, chairs and candelabra was aimed at. The style can be seen in Sheraton's *Cabinet-makers' and Upholsterers' Drawing Book* (1791-1794) and is fully developed in his *Cabinet Dictionary* issued a few years later. A gifted exponent of its most graceful phase was the architect, Henry Holland, and after his death in 1806 the leading influence was that of the amateur and virtuoso, Thomas Hope (1769-1831), whose designs in his *Household Furniture* (1807) were imitated by cabinet-makers. In this work Hope experimented in the Egyptian taste, to furnish a room in his country house in which Egyptian antiquities were housed.

In Regency furniture, designers aimed at simplicity of form, unbroken lines and bold curves, and the reduction of carved ornament to a minor role. With the disuse of carving and inlay in wood, stress was laid upon the employment of cabinet woods, such as rosewood, kingwood, calamander wood and zebrawood veneers having a marked figure. Painting was laid aside as less durable than applications and inlays of metal. English cabinet-makers made considerable use of inlay

[1] 1751-1806.
[2] R. Edwards and M. Jourdain, *Georgian Cabinet-makers*, p. 62.
[3] A. Alison, *Essays on Taste* (ed. 1825, Vol. 1. p. 368).

151

of brass, which was contrasted with a ground of dark wood. Cast brass colonettes and other details were also used to a considerable extent; and Sheraton notes in his *Cabinet Dictionary* the use of metal cock beads as an innovation.

II

WOODWORK AND CONSTRUCTION

ADVERTISEMENTS of the sale of mahogany planks and mahogany furniture
appear in journals from about 1723 onwards; and the first entry of its use
by cabinet-makers in the Royal Household accounts dates from 1724. The
new wood, which came into use as a fashionable and expensive novelty, was used
almost entirely in solid work for seat furniture and for dining, tripod and card
tables. Reception and dining rooms were the first to be refurnished in this
fashionable wood, while walnut veneered chests of drawers, cabinets and bureaux
were still being made for bedrooms and the private apartments.

All varieties of mahogany shrink very little and warp and twist less than any
other kind of timber. The first timber to be imported was the so-called Spanish
brought from the island of San Domingo lying to the east of Cuba, where forests
near the coast contained timber of great age. Very similar was the mahogany
obtained from the neighbouring islands of Cuba, Puerto Rico and Jamaica, on
which the high rocky soil had produced trees of very slow growth, which in consequence were close in the grain. This wood was dark and rich in colour; the San
Domingo had very little figure, but that from the other islands was often better
marked. When seasoned, such wood proved difficult to work, and necessitated
tools of steel of the best quality, sharpened to great keenness. This hard mahogany
acquires a polish by the process of planing the surface. Carving in Spanish
mahogany shows a crispness comparable with chased metal. The skilled workman
was able to cut his mortices and tenons with such accuracy that when fitting them
together the air was imprisoned in the cavity, and finally escaped with a rush.

Towards the middle of the century there was a large demand for case-
furniture, such as chests of drawers, cabinets, bookcases, which brought into play
the art of veneering. Cuban wood was mostly cut for veneers, and several varieties
of figure were obtained. The period when figured mahogany was sought after must
be dated soon after 1750. The range of figure to be found in mahogany is very

wide. The most commonly found is the plain stripe, shown in wood cut on the quarter. Fiddle-back figure is found chiefly on the outside edges of Honduras mahogany. The term 'plum mottle' is descriptive of a figure showing dark, elliptical marks. 'Roe' is a term given to dark flakes in a figure, which give a fine effect of light and shade. 'Stopped' or 'broken' mottles consist of 'flame like marks and irregular figures of varying and spreading forms'. A variety of mahogany (known as baywood) imported in the second half of the eighteenth century came from forests on the coast of Honduras in Central America. It is a tree of quicker growth, and is much lighter in weight and colour; the grain is open and straight and the wood is easy to work and when used was generally stained. Polishing took very much longer for Honduras wood, than for Spanish or Cuban.

The finest red pine was usually the base for veneering and the veneer was laid in larger pieces than had been general in walnut. A whole panel, for instance, would be faced with one sheet of veneer. Panels were often halved and quartered. The feather or herring-bone borders were no longer attempted, and cross-banding was not general before 1765, after which in addition to its use as a narrow border it was also employed in facing the frames of glazed doors, and on panels forming the surround of a centrally placed oval of vertical figure edged with holly or box lines. This late cross-banding is always mitred at the corners.

Mouldings in mahogany were run with the grain (by a moulding plane before they were fixed) and fixed by glue and panel pins. They were built up of short lengths only when working around quick curves such as the cornices of bow-fronted corner cupboards. Small mouldings were bent to curves by steaming. Mouldings in mahogany were frequently carved up till about 1775.

Satinwood had a great vogue in the reign of George III and much fashionable furniture (chairs, settees, card tables, occasional tables and cabinets) was constructed in or faced with this East Indian importation. It was polished to enhance its light yellow tone. It was soon discovered that certain cuts of chestnut veneers would give a somewhat similar effect; and coloured birch was also used to imitate satinwood. Woods of native growth employed in veneering were pollarded walnut, oak and elm; the burrs of walnut and elm; sycamore, chestnut, box, yew, holly, harewood[1] (dyed sycamore), beech, pear, cherry and laburnum.

Among imported woods were satinwood, tulipwood, kingwood, amboyna, thuya, rosewood, zebrawood and snakewood.

Some pieces made of the hardest Spanish mahogany were left untouched by varnish, oil or wax. Others were treated with poppy or linseed oil, or were

[1] Sycamore, when stained, turns after exposure to a brownish grey colour.

beeswaxed. When Honduras wood was employed, the more open and softer grain needed a longer treatment. One method was to use powdered brickdust with linseed oil under a pad, which by continual rubbing produced a fine hard-wearing polish. Frequently the oil was dyed with alkanet root. When beeswax was used, the surfaces were usually first treated with two or three coats of gum lac dissolved in spirit, which sank into and filled the grain, making it easier to get a rich polish with the wax. In using the wax on chairs and over carving it was applied with a rather stiff brush and also polished with a brush. In a fine quality varnish several coats were applied at intervals and a polish was obtained by rubbing the surfaces with rotten-stone and oil with the palm of the hand.

The brass handles, drawer pulls and escutcheons of the mahogany period underwent many changes. From 1715 to 1735 the slender drop loop on a shaped back plate, either pierced or solid, was retained. About 1740 the drop loop became stouter and was shaped like a bird's beak against each bolt head. About the middle years of the eighteenth century a new fixing was given to the loop handle by substituting two small oval or circular plates for the single linking plate. This pattern is found throughout the second half of the century and is figured in its latest phases in trade lists for stamped back plates, dating from about 1790 to 1810.

The fashion of using key escutcheons of the same shapes as the back plates to the handles ceased about 1730 and after this date the keyhole was usually edged by a brass rim driven in flush and known as a thread escutcheon. These were used throughout the remainder of the century. When ornate French handles were employed, however, chased escutcheons frequently accompanied them.

In 1777 a Birmingham brassfounder, John Marston, improved upon a process of stamping brass goods invented in 1769, and applied it successfully to furniture fittings. After this date the back plates of drawer pulls, which were of oval, circular, and octagonal outline, were ornamented and moulded by stamping thin sheet brass so that it appeared hollow at the back. Other late types were knob shapes having a stamped face, such as a wreath of flowers, or a lion's head, and fitted with a screw or bolt for securing to the wood.

Turned mahogany knobs appeared about 1800, either fitted with a brass screw or set in a stamped brass cup to which a bolt was attached. The mahogany knobs with wood screws found on many drawers are Victorian substitutions.

III

JAPANNING

There was a revival of japanning in the middle years of the eighteenth century, and a book of designs, the *Ladies' Amusement, or the Whole Art or Japanning Made Easy*, containing upwards of fifteen hundred designs, was evidently directed at the amateur japanner. It is stated in the preface that the art 'had prevailed much of late'. In the instructions to the reader it is recommended to apply several coats of varnish to form the ground, but there is no mention of a priming of size and whiting. In a later treatise, *The Artists' Arcanum* (1799) 'japanning in the modern way' is described as 'simply consisting of beginning and finishing with varnish'.

The most fashionable japanned object was the cabinet upon a stand, the latter being of side table form, but carved on the legs and frieze and entirely gilt. Stands more simply decorated were often finished in japanning. Between 1740 and 1750 the cabinets became taller, and were sometimes designed with crestings. The brass work lost its important position early in George III's reign and consisted merely of a small key escutcheon and plain brass butts hidden in the joints of the doors. Examples of japanning are found as late as 1770 on furniture designed by Robert Adam for Osterley and Nostell, but the art of japanning had degenerated by 1788 into painting furniture in varnish colours.[1] The ornamental detail usually bore no reference to oriental originals.

Illustrations on page 115.

[1] In the *Guide* (1788) Japanning is described as 'a new fashion which has arisen within these few years'.

IV

GESSO

THE decoration of furniture by means of gesso came in as an adjunct to the gilding. Soft woods (chiefly deal) were used as a basis; and the surface was treated with whiting and size to form a ground, upon which the same mixture was laid on, following the lines of a traced pattern; when set, the ornament was dressed down with sharp scraping tools. Parts in strong relief were carved in wood glued to the surface, and then thinly coated with the composition. The whole surface was gilt. The ground was often sanded before gilding or punched after that process to give it matt surface. This treatment was applied mostly to side tables, stands, and to mirror frames, for which it was suitable. In walnut seat furniture small panels of gesso-work were sometimes inserted in the splats and on the legs. There was a vogue for gesso from about 1700 to 1725 for furniture for ceremonial use; and the frequent use of armorial details and cyphers indicate that it was specially ordered by clients. After its decline as decoration for tables, stands and seat-furniture, gesso continued in use for the frames of mirrors.

Illustrations on pages 140, 201 and 223.

V

CHAIRS

THE earliest specimens of mahogany chairs are indistinguishable from those of the late walnut fashions, except in their colour and the absence of veneering. The cabriole leg with club foot that had proved so satisfactory in walnut, was retained in mahogany on simple designs. For the finer specimens, the foot was carved as a bird's claw clasping a ball, or as a lion's paw; and from about 1725 to 1740 the knee was sometimes carved with the lion or satyr mask, or the shell and pendant. The terminals of the arms were carved with heads.

When the earlier solid splat was discarded for one of open design the piercing was plain at first, consisting of a series of narrow vertical cuts, leaving about five slender uprights grouped in the centre. This splat was framed into the shoe on the top of the back seat rail and into the under side of the top rail, which, though still shaped, was becoming less arched or hooped, and also almost squared at the corner junctions with the back uprights. Later the splat was daringly pierced, and often carved in a variety of patterns, though in many cases the outline is reminiscent of the solid vase and fiddle-shaped walnut splats. The hoop form of back was not entirely dropped, but in the majority the uprights were without the break just above the seat frame, and continued with a gradual outward curve to the top rail, where the back was widest. Below the seat frame the rear legs gradually converged to the floor; viewed sideways, the complete outline of legs with the uprights shows the extremities well to the rear of the seat frame. This involved a rather complicated setting out in shaping those members, and required accurate templates for both faces in addition to a large piece of mahogany.

Caning[1] was 'almost out of use' in 1747 and entirely obsolete in 1761; but the stuffing and covering of seat furniture was developed. In the early Georgian period the seat was stuffed over and the backs stuffed in, with the uprights and

[1] *The London Tradesman* (1747) and Collyer's *The Parents and Guardians' Directory* (1761).

top rail exposed. Frequently the legs were of scroll shape with flat side face. The face of the leg was carved, and in some rare instances swags of fruit and flowers were arranged between the legs on front and side. On some chairs the square tapering leg with moulded plinth was adopted; in such cases the arm supports rise from the front corners and curve backwards as they rise to the horizontal arms.

The seat frame, usually very deep and exposed beneath the material, was carved with classic detail. The chairs with square or cabriole legs were invariably either of walnut or mahogany upon which the enrichment was occasionally gilded. Those of richer design, with bold carving and scroll legs, were generally of soft wood with surfaces prepared with a coating of size and whiting and gilt.

During the rococo period, from about 1740, carving was low in relief, the acanthus was scroll-like in its form, and the leaf spikes were finished with a twist. The acanthus was employed to enrich all parts of the open-work back as well as the knees of the legs; this carving was executed with great skill, and was varied in scale. The splat was often pierced to represent a balanced group of C scrolls interlaced with flat strap work. In some examples the splat was left solid in the upper half. The two types of arms used on late walnut chairs were still popular, the shaped supports rising from the side rails of the seat frame a few inches behind the front corners. From about 1745 to 1760 the plainer mahogany chairs retained the simple strap work and C-scroll splats, sometimes enriched with rococo ornament on the faces and the shaped top rail. In such chairs the legs were of plain cabriole shapes until about 1755. The seat was either on a separate drop-in frame or stuffed over. About 1755 the less expensive straight square leg came in, but did not supersede the cabriole. The cabriole leg was sometimes carved with mouldings accentuating its curvature, and these were broken in places by excrescences of small leaf scrolls, which were also worked in great variety on the shoulder-pieces and frequently carried across the seat frame on a scroll outline. Amongst the ornament derived from France was the cabochon, of irregular cartouche form.

The pierced splat developed into a variety of intertwining patterns. One design, illustrated in the *Director* (1754), is the ribbon treatment, which was enriched with scrolls and leaf carving. In some examples the splat is united with the side uprights. The curves were arranged to sweep up into the top rail and to appear to be all cut from a single plank of mahogany; careful inspection, however, will reveal the perfect jointing. These apparently delicate splats are remarkably strong, the effect of lightness being obtained by cutting back the return faces of each member so that they are narrower at the back. The piercings were cut out with a fret-saw and the rear arrises trimmed off with a chisel; when this was done

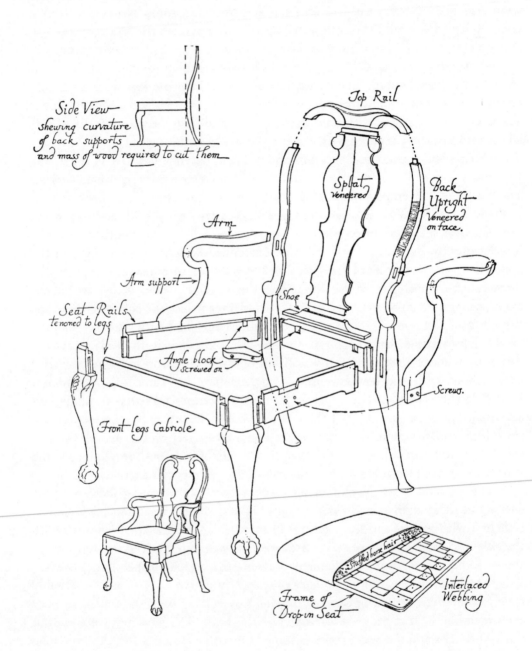

Side View
shewing curvature
of back supports
and mass of wood required to cut them

Top Rail

Splat
veneered

Back
Upright
veneered
on face.

Arm

Arm support

Shoe

Seat Rails
tenoned to legs

Angle block
screwed on

Screws.

Front Legs Cabriole

Stuffed horse hair

Interlaced
Webbing

Frame of
Drop-in Seat

J.C. ROGERS. Mens et Delt:

the tool marks were left, forming a contrast to the finish of the front of the splat. The types of seat-frame shaping continued in use so long as the cabriole leg was employed; but with the adoption of the square leg the corners of the seat frame were squared, the sides tapered to the back, and the front was straight or serpentine.

The cabriole leg was revived about 1780 on chairs of French type. Stretchers reappeared in some cases in the middle of the eighteenth century. For their reintroduction there is no satisfactory explanation; on structural grounds they had long been considered superfluous, yet they reappeared on chairs of Gothic and Chinese taste and between cabriole as well as the square legs. They were of simple rectangular section, about five-eighths of an inch wide and one and a quarter inches deep. With the general use of the square leg the stretchers were always present, but those on Gothic chairs were frequently widely chamfered with stops to leave a normal section at the joints.

In the 'Chinese' chairs the back and also the spaces enclosed by the arms and their supports were filled with large scale frets. On some examples the top rail was shaped to represent a pagoda roof. The arm panels invariably leant outward at an angle, which necessitated an inward curve at the rear of the arm in order to meet and frame into the side of the back upright. The legs were generally square, the front pair perfectly vertical and footed with small plinth blocks; they were either left solid, hollowed out on the inner angle, or built up. When solid, they were often enriched with a low relief fret carved up the two outer faces, a treatment termed card-cut ornament. When the legs were hollowed out or built up the outer faces were pierced with similar frets, and often appear fragile. A turned shaft was in some cases set in the hollow leg, which in section was L-shaped, the shaft occupying the angle between the arms of the L. Fret-cut brackets were usual in the angles between the legs and seat frame, the latter being sometimes faced with a strip of mahogany, card cut or pierced with frets.

The stretchers were of the plain rectangular section, frequently fret-cut. The trellis panels of the back and beneath the arms were either fret-sawn out of one board or were built up.

A well-known design is the 'ladder-back', which appears after 1760. In this the slightly undulating top rail is repeated in three or four rails at lower levels framed into the back uprights. In the best examples the top and ladder rails were carved with narrow scrolls and leaf edging bordering slight piercings. In the plain country ladder-backs the carving was omitted and the piercings, if present, enlarged. Such chairs had square legs, often with a wave-moulded surface on the two outer faces of the front pair, and four plain stretchers. The seat was stuffed over the rails or on a drop-in frame, and was frequently dipped.

The moulding worked on the leg faces was often repeated on the back uprights and the arm supports, but it is not uncommon to find it present on the back members, while the legs are plain but for a tiny ovolo worked on the outer arris. This latter moulding is also found carved in rope and bead patterns, and appears on chairs with pierced and carved splats.

In the early specimens of upholstered chairs in walnut and in mahogany the plain stuffed-over back and seat was continued. The wood of the arms was on many entirely exposed, but a frequent practice was to stuff or pad the horizontal member, leaving the support exposed. To suit the dimensions of ladies' dresses, the arm support was swept rapidly backward as it rose to the arm.

Single chairs were designed with wide seats, but in upholstered chairs the seat was broader and deeper. A distinct type of chair was introduced about 1720 for writing. The usual design had a square seat, two sides of which were open while the other two were enclosed by turned uprights rising from three of the legs. The tops of the uprights were connected by a horizontal built-up rail, semi-circular in plan, and about twelve inches above the seat. This had a flat top surface, and on the centre third of its length was thickened or covered with a shaped block, rounded off to give comfortable support. The two ends of the top rail were finished either in a plain horizontal scroll or scrolled over and carved. The two spaces between the three uprights were filled with shaped, pierced, and carved splats rising from the shoe-pieces. The seat was upholstered on a drop-in frame. The legs varied in design and arrangement. Usually all four legs were square, with the tiny ovolo running up the outer arris, and with plain stretchers crossing at right angles. Fine examples had all four legs cabriole; others had the one leg under the front corner of the seat cabrioled, while the remaining three legs were squared or taper-turned with pad feet. Soon after 1765 the influence of Robert Adam began to make itself felt among chair makers. At first he was guided by earlier models, as in the set of seat furniture from 19 Arlington Street, where the curvilinear form is retained though the decoration consists of classic detail. The drawing for this set is dated 1764; and the rapid development of Adam's taste is shown in a set made for Moor Park five years later,[1] which 'in severity and line and delicacy of ornament anticipates later developments and recalls a type fashionable in France under Louis XVI'. On his chairs he usually placed the square tapering leg, which, at the level of the seat rail, had an oval patera carved in a sunk panel or applied. A cavetto

[1] *Dictionary of English Furniture*, Vol. III, p. 99. The settee of this set is illustrated, *ibid.*, p. 104.

mould was cut on all faces of the leg immediately below the seat, and upon the uninterrupted taper simple flutes were cut which stopped just above a moulded plinth cut in the solid. Seat rails were moulded when not stuffed over. Chairs of this period were often inlaid with delicate classical detail, or when made in beech were painted with similar motifs.

For upholstered chairs Adam largely designed on French lines, with an oval-back frame of moulded wood stuffed in, and upholstered, together with the seat, in material patterned with classical detail. The seat was oval or circular and stuffed over, yet showing a moulded lower frame running into square blocks at the tops of the legs. The oval back frame was held by tenons on the short moulded continuations of the turned rear legs. The front legs were also taper-turned, but above the seat-rail they rose in square section, serpentine-curved, to support horizontal bowed arms which had padded tops. These arm supports and the legs were fluted, the latter terminating in small, swell-turned feet. Such chairs were generally beech, gilt or painted.

The majority of chair backs figured in Heppelwhites' *Guide* derived their support from the upward continuation of the back legs, and dispensed with a splat connected to the seat. Some examples, however, retained the earlier treatment. The favourite back shapes in the *Guide* were the shield, the oval, and the heart, with various open-work splats[1]; every member being of curved work necessitated the utmost care in selecting the wood and perfect construction. The faces were slightly sunk or moulded, and carving in low relief with motifs such as the husk, honeysuckle, wheatear, palmette, and other simple leaf forms was placed in well-considered positions. The Prince of Wales's feathers were also present on chairs of this period. In certain forms of chair backs, such as three interlaced ovals, the jointing and direction of the grain was obscured by a cross-banded veneer of mahogany on the front face. Generally, the legs tapered slightly and were of square section. Taper legs were fluted or panel-sunk, with plinth feet. Another type of this style of leg was turned and fluted in the French manner; and where these occur on armchairs the arm supports are invariably turned.

Seats continued to be stuffed over or on a drop-in frame. The favourite covering materials were horsehair and mohair cloths, and silks; and when stuffed over the rails, brass-headed nails were a usual edge fixing.

Whereas in the earlier mahogany chairs the arm supports invariably rose from and were screwed to the side rails of the seat, on many of Adam and Hepplewhite

[1] In the case of the oval back, the splat was contained within the oval and was not connected with the seat rail.

type they carry up from the front legs just an inch or two above the seat, when they suddenly sweep backwards and up to the shaped arm in a long concave curve; in other cases the arm support remained serpentine in shape.

The rectangular square-cornered back shape was used during the Hepple-white period with a row of vertical bars for a filling, but the finer chairs were made with the top rail ramped at each side, the centre portion being a narrow horizontal panel. In such chairs the splat work was restrained, consisting of a set of narrow bars with formal loops of drapery which rose from a low cross-rail a few inches above the seat. Many chairs were made for drawing-rooms and bedrooms in beech, entirely covered with a painted or japanned ground, and ornamented with sprays, husk lines, paterae, and other ornaments, painted or gilt.

Chairs of Sheraton design were produced in great variety. Generally, as regards the treatment of the back, he did not repeat the shield and heart shapes, but reproduced the rectangular forms, lightening them still further with various semi-classic splats or cross rails, often inlaid and delicately carved. Some top rails were turned, and these were generally accompanied by uprights that scroll back at the top. A variation of the splat was a filling of trellis bars; also, between pairs of horizontal bars, rows of small balls or pierced circles were placed. Another type with caned seat had caned panels in oval or rectangular frames inserted in the back. The arms did not join the back uprights squarely, but swept up to join the upright near its top. When the arm support was shaped as a concave curve rising above a square leg the junction with the arm was angular, but the majority of Sheraton arms were of S shape (to side view), and rose from a turned extension of a taper-turned and moulded front leg. These S arms, when viewed from above, are found to curve in serpentine form, which obviated what would otherwise have been an awkward-looking joint with the back upright, owing to the front of the seat being wider than the back. After about 1800 the S arms were reeded on the upper surface, and the uprights were also reeded.

On chairs of light construction the rear legs were turned; on dining chairs they were rectangular and curved well backwards, but were devoid of the curves on the transverse plane.

It is important to notice the character of eighteenth century turning. During the early and middle mahogany period it had no place in fashionable work, ex-cepting for the stems of tripods, but Robert Adam employed it throughout his career. During the periods of Hepplewhite and Sheraton turning became still more delicate, all curves being remarkably flat, and fillets and astragals, often minute, being kept strictly to proportion. These qualities should always be looked for in the work of the last thirty years of the eighteenth century, and when compared with the turning of 1820 and onwards the difference is so great as to suggest a lapse of a century instead of merely twenty years.

From about 1800 the top rail of the chair back was often cut out of a rectangular strip about four inches wide, and rode over the back uprights, on to which it was fixed by tapering dovetails slotted into the back. This late top rail was generally enriched with a sunk moulded border, a feature also applied to the lower cross-bars of the back.

Some fine chairs in the Sheraton styles were constructed in solid satinwood, and they were frequently inlaid and painted. Various leg stretchers were used, particularly on painted chairs, but the majority of late mahogany chairs were without them.

A favourite pattern with Regency chairs was to shape the front legs in bold concave curves, with a gradual taper and projecting forwards to balance the rearward curves of the back legs. At the sides the legs and seat frame were quite flush, the latter being dipped and forming one continuous curve with the knee of the front leg and the bow of the back upright without break in the line. The uprights usually scrolled over at the top, and were connected by flat or turned cross-members, the former often inlaid or faced with brass ornament, and the latter enriched with a spiral reeding or rope twist. Many turned cross-bars are concave to the back, but as the grain remain straight the ends must have been turned in separate operations, sufficient stuff having been allowed to shift the lathe centres. The centre part was twist turned, or moulded. Seats were generally caned and fitted with a squab cushion. When arms were fitted, a general design was the S-shape, but instead of the turned support the arm curved down in a circular arc, which just touched the seat frame and continued to finish in a small scroll. This was weak construction, as it was impossible to avoid short cross-grain at the front curve of the arm, nor possible to obtain a thoroughly secure joint with the seat frame. Other arms were straight with a scroll-over termination, which was capped on a concave support, both being fluted or reeded; they were generally accompanied by legs which had squares faced with paterae at the seat frame, and were taper turned and reeded. In some cases seats and backs were upholstered.

In addition to many chairs in mahogany or rosewood, many were made in beech, painted and gilded.

A distinctive chair made in and near London in the eighteenth century was the Windsor, which was a cheap and serviceable seat much used as a garden seat, in tea gardens, and in inns and public houses.

This chair was made by the turner, not by the joiner. After the seat is shaped by the adze and smoothed, holes are bored in it for the legs and back to fit in. The legs and back are hammered into these holes; and the legs often strengthened by stretchers. There are various forms of back; in the case of the bow-shaped back the wood is steamed until pliable, and then pulled into shape round an iron block and clamped until set.

Illustrations on pages 202-208.

VI

SETTEES AND SOFAS

URING the early Georgian period settees, which were of two types, varied
little from the late specimens of the walnut period.

The type with back composed of two or more chair backs continued
to be made throughout the eighteenth century, and specimens may be dated
according to the correspondence with the designs of contemporary chairs.

The second type was the elongation or widening of the upholstered chair.
The backs were stuffed over, and when high were generally straight. When the
back was lower the top line was serpentine or undulating, and was often swept in
with the arms. In many cases the seat frame was exposed and carved; other
specimens had the back stuffed within a shaped frame, which, together with the
arms, seat frame, and legs, was carved and gilt.

The arms were either solid-stuffed, or had a pad on the horizontal member,
with the forward end and support exposed. From the middle years of the eighteenth
century rococo ornament was freely employed, together with such motifs as
small acanthus, short scrolls, and gadrooned edging. Many settees were very long
and frequently had four front legs. The shaped top rail of the back and the front
face of the arms were left exposed and carved to accord with the enrichment of
the seat framing.

The French influence on design is shown in two upholstered couches which
are figured in the *Director* and described as 'what the French call *péché mortel*'. These
are 'something made to take asunder on the middle; one part makes a large
easy chair, and the other a stool'.

Composite pieces of furniture, of which the design was borrowed from
France, the 'confidente' and the 'duchesse', are illustrated and described in late
Georgian trade catalogues. The *confidente* was a sofa with two removable ends,
which could serve as arm chairs, the *duchesse* a stool with two removable ends
forming, when removed, arm chairs.

Beech was the usual wood used in building up the frame-work, mahogany being employed only for exposed parts when entire gilding was not intended.

The revived classic manner set the taste for the remainder of the eighteenth century and was adapted to the chair-back types and those with upholstered backs and seats. Some were veneered in satinwood with mahogany or tulip cross-banded borders. Settees of the Regency period were made *en suite* with a set of chairs. There was also a return to the couch of day-bed type, termed a 'Grecian couch', in which a low upholstered back was carried into a high roll-over end with the front face exposed in moulded and scrolled mahogany. In design these couches closely followed Roman models, the legs were either short and top-shaped, or curved outward.

Illustrations on pages 210 and 211.

VII

CHESTS OF DRAWERS

CHESTS of drawers, which remained of plain rectangular form when made in solid mahogany from about 1730, usually contained four or five drawers of the full width, and stood upon bracket feet, or occasionally upon short cabriole legs. A tall and narrow chest was made which might be termed a tallboy, but, unlike the usual type, the carcase was in one piece. In the second half of the century the chests were often taller and contained five or six drawers, two of them of half width placed at the top. The carcase was usually of pine, veneered, and framed by continuous dovetailing along all four angles of sides with bottom and top. The divisions between the drawers were solid from front to back, framed into grooves in the sides, and faced with mahogany strip or veneer.

The drawer linings were of fine quality oak, quarter sawn, and in some late eighteenth century examples the linings were of mahogany or of pine. When the chest was flat-fronted the drawer fronts were either of solid mahogany, or curl mahogany veneered on plain Honduras, oak or pine; but when the front was bow or serpentine, the drawer fronts were veneered on mahogany or pine shapes (usually the latter). A plinth mould projected at the base, and a smaller moulding surrounded the top edge, both of which, in fine examples, were carved.

The bottoms of small and narrow drawers throughout the period were in one piece, with grain running from front to back, and housed in grooves cut in the sides about quarter of an inch above the bottom edge. This arrangement was also used for the large, full-width drawers up to a very late date in the century. A new method, introduced about 1775, consisted of dividing the bottom into two panels by a central bearer running from front to back and grooved on each side to take the panel edges. These panels were thin and generally arranged with the grain running transversely. This method ensured the drawer, when loaded, would bear only on the side runners, and obviated sagging in the middle. The backs of carcases were often panelled, but the majority found to-day have the back enclosed by boarding nailed into the rebated sides and top. A minor difference from the practice of the walnut period was the provision of a face strip above the top drawers and below the bottom drawer, by which means all drawers appeared surrounded and separated by a narrow facing of the carcase.

The projecting lip mould of walnut type is found around many early mahogany drawer edges, but is invariably part of the actual solid front, and consequently is worked across the grain at the ends. The applied projecting cock bead was used after 1745 almost exclusively, and remained in use for the rest of the century.

The classic, French, Gothic and Chinese tastes found expression on chests of drawers, though it was restrained, as the drawer fronts were left plain save for the handles. The enrichment was worked on the top and plinth moulds, and on the bracket feet. The divisions between the drawers were also sometimes faced with carved mouldings, and on fine chests of serpentine shape the corners were treated as narrow pilasters arranged across the angle and covered with applied carving or frets.

The chest of drawers intended for use in reception rooms followed the French commode; and many of the period are influenced by contemporary French specimens. They were serpentine on front and sides, often with swelled contour on the drawer faces or the pair of doors which in some cases enclosed the drawers; the front corners were framed with long cabriole-shaped posts finishing in a scroll foot. The bottom was also shaped and carved.

Plain mahogany chests of drawers continued to be made throughout the second half of the century and into the nineteenth, both veneered and in solid mahogany; the bracket foot and plinth was retained, but about 1770 a French method was adopted, in which the plinth was omitted and the vertical corners carried down to the floor with a delicate outward curve at the base. With this form the bottom line of the framing is invariably shaped. From the first quarter of the eighteenth century a writing slide provided with small brass drop loops was fitted above the top drawer to many low chests.

About 1765 this was discontinued, and the top-drawer front was hinged at the bottom edge, which (by means of a brass quadrant working in a guide at each side) could be swung out to a horizontal position to serve as a writing flap. The whole drawer, fitted with pigeon-holes and small drawers, also pulled forward.

During the satinwood period many fine chests were veneered in this yellow wood, decorated with inlays and with painting.

Late eighteenth-century chests were in some cases very tall, sometimes had reeded quarter-columns let in on the front corners. A cross-banded edge to the top

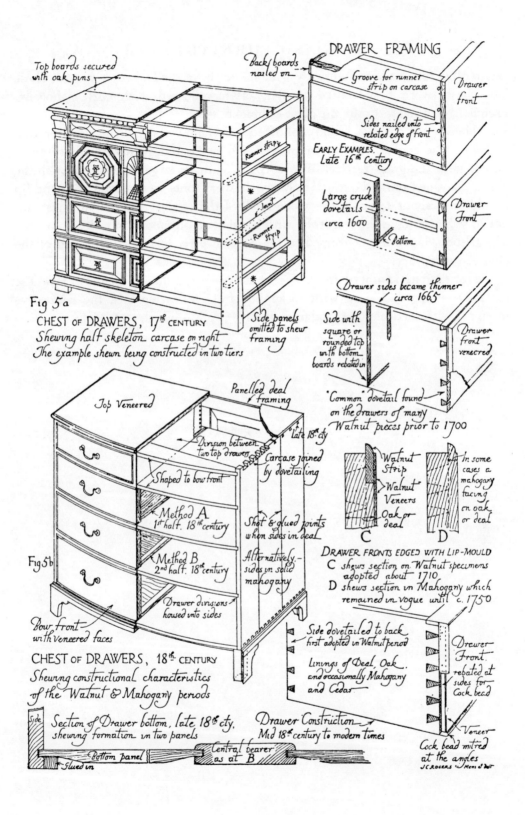

Top boards secured with oak pins

Back boards nailed on

DRAWER FRAMING

Groove for runner strip on carcase

Drawer front

Runner strip

Joint

Runner strip

Sides nailed into rebated edge of front

EARLY EXAMPLES.
Late 16th Century

Large crude dovetails circa 1600

Drawer front

Bottom

Fig 5a

CHEST of DRAWERS, 17th CENTURY
Shewing half skeleton carcase on right
The example shewn being constructed in two tiers

Side panels omitted to shew framing

Drawer sides became thinner circa 1665

Side with square or rounded top with bottom boards rebated in

Drawer front veneered

"Common" dovetail found on the drawers of many Walnut pieces prior to 1700

Top Veneered

Panelled deal framing

Late 18th cty

Division between two top drawers

Carcase joined by dovetailing

Shaped to bow front

Method A
1st half 18th century

Shot & glued joints when sides in deal

Method B
2nd half 18th century

Alternatively - sides in solid mahogany

Walnut Strip
Walnut Veneers
Oak or deal

In some cases a mahogany facing on oak or deal

C   D

Fig 5b

DRAWER FRONTS EDGED WITH LIP-MOULD
C shews section on Walnut specimens adopted about 1710
D shews section in Mahogany which remained in vogue until c. 1750

Bow front with veneered faces

Drawer divisions housed into sides

CHEST of DRAWERS, 18th CENTURY
Shewing constructional characteristics
of the Walnut & Mahogany periods

Side dovetailed to back first adopted in Walnut period

Linings of Deal, Oak and occasionally Mahogany and Cedar

Drawer Front rebated at sides for Cock bead

Side

Section of Drawer bottom, late 18th cty shewing formation in two panels

Bottom panel
Glued in

Central bearer as at B

Drawer Construction
Mid 18th century to modern times

Veneer

Cock bead mitred at the angles

J C ROGERS Mem S Dett

is also often found and an unusually wide frieze above the two top drawers. These late chests were bow-fronted or flat, often veneered with curl mahogany. Frequently turned feet took the place of bracket feet.

The double chest or tallboy followed late walnut designs with no alteration of form. The angles were often splayed and decorated with applied frets; or fluted, with the grain vertical. The cornice, with its large cavetto run with the grain, remained until about 1735. Many drawer fronts were edged with the lip mould until about 1745. In the second half of the century the double chest was not so fashionable, as the wardrobe with hanging accommodation was then in use. The tallboy, however, continued to be made in early form until the end of the eighteenth century.

Distinctions appeared in the cornice treatment shortly before 1750, the flat frieze being decorated with an applied fret; following this, the frieze was often cut with vertical flutes, and from about 1780 was inlaid.

Illustration on page 219.

VIII

BUREAUX

FOR many years after mahogany was in use bureaux followed closely the design of walnut examples, but mirror plates were no longer fitted on the door panels. In some cases pilasters with carved caps and moulded bases were fitted to the door stiles. This treatment became lighter about 1740, and from this date until about 1750 the panels were framed with a wavy inner edge on the stiles and rails, or the panel was framed in flush, veneered over the whole surface, and a panel effect obtained by planting on a narrow mould of wavy contour with applied carved acanthus sprays at the four angles. This latter arrangement continued until *circa* 1760.

The cornice, though still classic, was proportioned on a smaller scale, and a dentil course was generally present. On fine specimens a pierced cresting board was fixed, but this was discarded soon after 1750 and the broken pediment again became universal, the form of the pediment being angular, circular, curved, or of swan-neck form. From about 1765 the section with an oblique flap on the lower stage became outmoded. Henceforth designed as a flat chest of drawers, the top drawer of this secretaire section pulls out a few inches. The drawer front swings down to stop at the horizontal, and is held rigid by a pair of brass quadrant stays.

The treatment of drawer fronts, plinth, and feet followed the variations of those members upon the chests of drawers, the cabriole-shaped bracket foot being in fashion between 1740 and 1755. The bureau interior was fitted with small drawers, pigeon-holes, and a central cupboard with flanking pilasters, which together formed a movable unit released by a hidden spring to disclose narrow pockets behind the pilasters. The sides were usually veneered in one piece; the flap had a veneer of picked curl figure and retained the lip moulded edge; the bracket feet were invariably cut from solid mahogany. Comparatively few bureaux of this type were made or faced with satinwood.

Mahogany bureaux dating from the last two decades of the eighteenth century retain the old form, but sometimes have the bracket feet connected by a serpentine

173

curve under the plinth mould. The drawer fronts and the flap were inlaid with borders, and often with an oval and shell in the centre of the latter.

Among variations in detail in the late eighteenth century was the substitution of a sliding cylindrical cover instead of the hinged slanting flap. This was introduced[1] between 1785 and 1790 and some specimens were made with a shallow drawer under the writing compartment and carried on slender taper legs. The sliding cover was a quarter cylinder constructed of segments of wood glued up to form the curve. This cover operated on being lifted by knobs at the bottom edge, and travelled upwards and inwards on side tracks to occupy a position behind the pigeon-holes. In some cases the cover was constructed on the tambour principle in which a series of slats, rounded on face, were glued side by side to a backing of stout coarse linen or fine canvas.

A feature dating from about 1785 was the attachment of turned and carved columns arranged in front of the pilaster strips which divided the doors and drawers of the lower part. In such cases the plinth was usually omitted, and the columns were carried down as turned feet.

Illustration on page 213.

[1] The *bureau à cylindre* was developed in France about 1750.

IX

BOOKCASES AND CABINETS

Both in bookcases and cabinets, the architectural character is pronounced during the early Georgian period, as might be expected from an age when even builders and carpenters 'took great pleasure in the study of architecture'.

The bookcase was the province of the architect; and for the guidance of clients the *City and Country Builders' and Workmens' Treasury of Designs* was issued by Batty Langley in 1740, containing a number of designs 'true after any one of the five orders. In these the entablature is often surmounted by an open pediment, allowing space for a bust or a vase'. Towards the middle of the eighteenth century the architectural tradition weakened. In the designs for bookcases in the *Director* the pediment which surmounts the advanced centres of winged bookcases is sometimes perforated and treated as continuous with a gallery.

Cabinets fitted with a number of adjustable shelves for books and with glazed doors were made in large numbers about the middle of the century, the doors, with some early exceptions, being divided by bars into panes. From about 1750 thin mahogany glazing bars were introduced; these were usually of astragal section not more than three-eighths of an inch wide, and composed of two parts. From about 1770 the door frames were often veneered with cross-banding and border lines of contrasting woods; also, from about this date, the lower or bed mould of the cornice was often a cavetto cut into a series of pointed arches which spring from small turned half pendants glued on the frieze. The backs of cabinets were generally panelled, at first with oak, and then with mahogany or pine. Cornices of cabinets and bookcases of the mahogany period were all more or less classic in profile and, being run by hand with small moulding planes, were of necessity worked in separate units or tiers, and built up in position one above the other.[1] Cabinet doors before 1750 invariably had the heavy ovolo-moulded

[1] This in modern work is rarely done, for with powerful moulding machines it is possible to cut the complete profile at one operation from a single board, which, when erected in a slanting position, give the same effect.

DEVELOPMENT IN GLAZING OF CABINET DOORS c1675-1800.

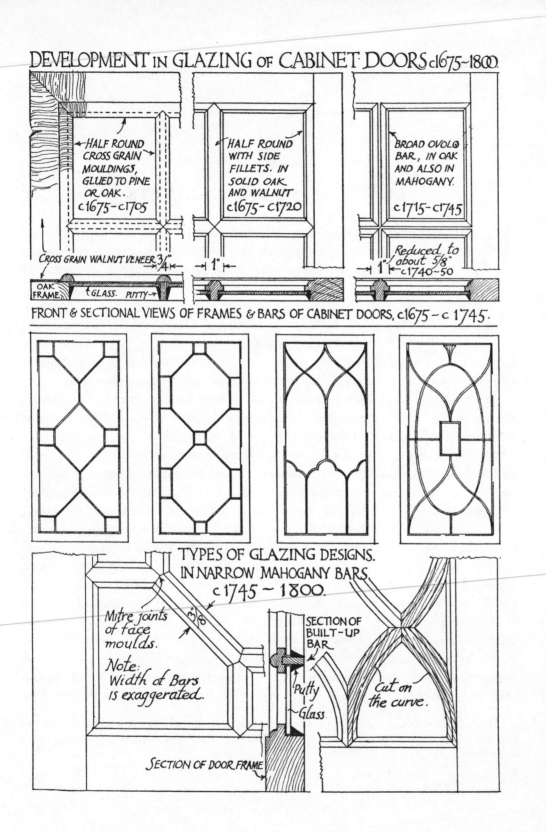

HALF ROUND CROSS GRAIN MOULDINGS, GLUED TO PINE OR OAK. c1675-c1705

HALF ROUND WITH SIDE FILLETS. IN SOLID OAK AND WALNUT c1675-c1720

BROAD OVOLO BAR, IN OAK AND ALSO IN MAHOGANY. c1715-c1745

Reduced to about 5/8" c1740-50

CROSS GRAIN WALNUT VENEER 3/4"   1"   1"

OAK FRAME   GLASS. PUTTY

FRONT & SECTIONAL VIEWS OF FRAMES & BARS OF CABINET DOORS, c1675-c1745.

TYPES OF GLAZING DESIGNS.
IN NARROW MAHOGANY BARS.
c1745-1800.

Mitre joints of face moulds.

Note: Width of Bars is exaggerated.

SECTION OF BUILT-UP BAR

Putty
Glass

Cut on the curve.

SECTION OF DOOR FRAME

glazing bars. The curved panel framing of 1740-1750 was also applied to glazed doors, with cross-bars of shaped outline.

Large china cabinets of the second half of the century were frequently designed with a break front (i.e. a centre section projecting slightly in front of two separate wing units) and made separately. Under the classical revival bookcases and cabinets returned to the architect's discipline. In the *Guide* (1788) the cornices of bookcases are sometimes surmounted by light foliations centring in an urn. In the last years of the century the great demand for bookcases among the increased reading public made them the 'leading article of employ' among some cabinet makers.[1] Both bookcases and cabinets were veneered with satinwood, but these are rare.

During the Regency period dwarf bookcases were introduced to leave the walls clear for paintings or prints. Many low bookcases and stands were also designed to 'contain all the books that may be desired for a sitting-room without reference to the library'.[2] A novelty was the bookcase or bookstand in which the shelves revolve round a central column or shaft, for which a patent was taken out in 1808. This form of bookstand, which is illustrated in Ackermann's *Repository* (1810) and described as 'an ingenious contrivance', could be placed in 'a recess, or corner of a room in which from local circumstances it might be inconvenient or impossible to display the same number of books'. Fixed graduated shelves at suitable distances were screwed to its central shaft, and each shelf was divided into compartments by cross pieces, the interior being filled up by dummy book fronts, 'or in any other ornamental way'.

Illustrations on pages 214-218.

[1] *Cabinet Dictionary* (1803), pp. 70-71.
[2] Ackermann's *Repository* (1823).

X

TABLES

The fashion of using a number of small dining tables declined during George I's reign, and reversion to the long table took place.

The gate-leg played the most important part in their construction, but it was of a new type. The oak gate-leg continued in use in country districts, but the fashionable gate table from early in George II's reign was made in mahogany or walnut, having four or six cabriole legs (two or four being fixed to a narrow rectangular under frame), and on each of the long sides an extra leg tenoned above the knee to the arm and pivoted by a wooden hinge on the main frame, swung out on an arm of the under frame. The top was usually oval or circular and composed of a central fixed board and two flaps, with an ovolo or ogee-moulded edge. The method of dowel fixing the table top was superseded by the metal screw. On the sides of the under frame, at regular intervals, slanting grooves were gouged out which provided a starting-point for screws, which were driven in until they entered the thickness of the top and held it securely in place. Likewise in the mortice and tenon joints of the framing the dowel pins were generally omitted, and hot thin glue was applied to the members composing the joint immediately before assembling and cramping up.

Some tables, in order to increase the maximum length, were composed of three units, the centre unit being a double gate table with rectangular flaps, on each side of which a semi-circular pier-type table could be fitted, thus providing a long table with semi-circular ends. The tops when placed together were fixed by brass clips and eyes. Dining tables for great establishments were built up on this unit principle. Many mahogany dining tables dating from the late eighteenth century were of beautifully figured wood with inlaid and cross-banded borders. About 1800 attempts were made to produce extending dining tables in which the leaves were detachable, and some ingenious devices were patented. The majority were worked by a sliding under frame, and additional flaps were inserted when the

GATE~LEG TABLES.

CONSTRUCTION AND — TYPE DIAGRAMS.

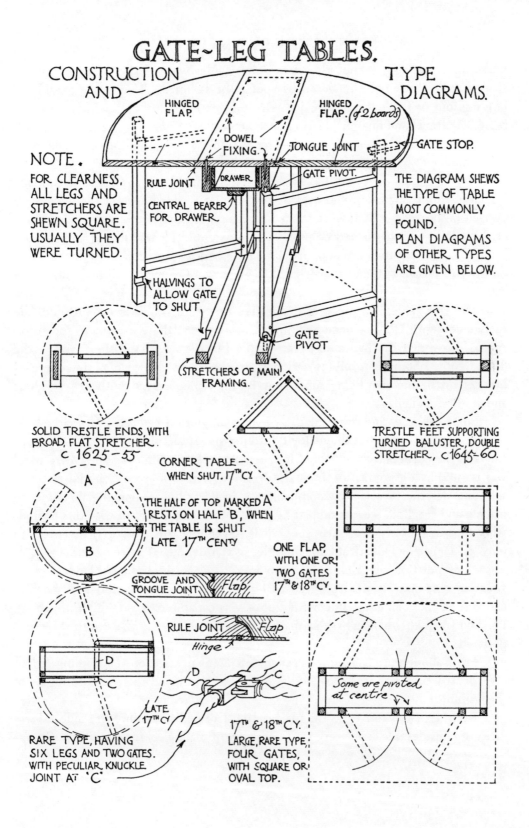

HINGED FLAP.

HINGED FLAP. (of 2 boards)

DOWEL FIXING.

TONGUE JOINT

GATE STOP.

RULE JOINT

DRAWER

GATE PIVOT.

CENTRAL BEARER FOR DRAWER

NOTE.
FOR CLEARNESS, ALL LEGS AND STRETCHERS ARE SHEWN SQUARE. USUALLY THEY WERE TURNED.

THE DIAGRAM SHEWS THE TYPE OF TABLE MOST COMMONLY FOUND. PLAN DIAGRAMS OF OTHER TYPES ARE GIVEN BELOW.

HALVINGS TO ALLOW GATE TO SHUT.

GATE PIVOT

STRETCHERS OF MAIN FRAMING.

SOLID TRESTLE ENDS, WITH BROAD, FLAT STRETCHER. c 1625-55

CORNER TABLE - WHEN SHUT. 17TH CY.

TRESTLE FEET SUPPORTING TURNED BALUSTER, DOUBLE STRETCHER, c 1645-60.

A

B

THE HALF OF TOP MARKED "A" RESTS ON HALF "B", WHEN THE TABLE IS SHUT. LATE 17TH CENTY

GROOVE AND TONGUE JOINT Flap

ONE FLAP, WITH ONE OR TWO GATES 17TH & 18TH CY.

RULE JOINT Flap
Hinge

D

C

D

C

LATE 17TH CY.

Some are pivoted at centre

RARE TYPE, HAVING SIX LEGS AND TWO GATES. WITH PECULIAR KNUCKLE JOINT AT "C"

17TH & 18TH CY. LARGE, RARE TYPE, FOUR GATES, WITH SQUARE OR OVAL TOP.

table was extended. About this date some tables were designed with lattice-shaped under framing, connected by special brass hinges. They were capable of holding four or five extra leaves, and when not extended, of collapsing into a side table, the travel and final disposition of the eight legs being an ingenious problem. During the classical influence the usual leg was the taper with plinth or spade foot; the turned leg was more frequent during the early nineteenth century.

Another type of dining table which dates from about 1790 was often made for large rooms. The top was oval or rectangular, reeded around the edge, and carried on bearers, which were hinged by means of pins to the rectangular block at the top of a stout turned column. The pins could be withdrawn and the top removed. The column was supported by four concave or serpentine legs reeded on the top surfaces; the extremities of the legs were capped with brass lion-claw castors.

The side table as a piece of decorative furniture which is a creation of the early eighteenth century occupied a position between the windows in reception rooms, furnished the hall and served as the forerunner of the sideboard in the dining room. Some side tables dating from the early Georgian period were of bracket form, the slab being supported by an eagle, carved with great vigour and vitality, and gilt.

Some tables dating from the early mahogany period had carved cabriole legs, wholly or parcel-gilt; but the majority had massive scroll-shape legs, placed either singly at the corners, or connected in truss forms. In certain cases the entire stand was treated as a composition in sculpture. The slab of marble, mosaic, slate or scagliola was the invariable accompaniment in great houses and the varieties of marble and scagliola were a subject of great interest to the *virtuosi* of this period, who ransacked Italy for rare specimens. Scagliola (or 'paste'), invented in Italy as a cheaper substitute for marble, was introduced here about 1735. It was a composition of calcined gypsum mixed with isinglass and Flanders glue; when in this state it was coloured to imitate the different varieties of marble, and laid on like cement; after hardening it was capable of a very high polish. In England fragments of Derbyshire marble were sometimes worked into the composition.

From about 1740 the lighter French detail was present on the framing, when the construction was in soft wood. Gilding was employed to cover the whole of the framing.

Between 1750 and 1760 the marble top declined in favour, and side tables, often of considerable size, were made entirely of mahogany for use in the dining-room. Great refinement marks the design of these tables during the period of the classical revival. The top was straight-fronted or serpentine; the frieze carved or fluted, the legs of square or round section, tapered and fluted. In some cases a pair of tables, each upon three legs and with quadrant shaped tops, were supplied to round off the ends of the side table.

Side or pier tables with semi-circular tops, which were made in large numbers from about 1770, were identical with contemporary card tables, except that the top was a fixture and all legs were immovable. Shaped stretchers appeared on some examples.

Centre tables were often used as tea tables. From about 1750 a fret-cut gallery was affixed to the edge of the square or serpentine top, and on some specimens this gallery formed the sides of a removable tray. Frequently much of the design was carried out in fret cutting, the legs having the two outer faces hollow or decorated with card cutting. The hollow legs sometimes enclosed a circular shaft rising from a solid plinth block within the angle.

In the Gothic taste, legs were built up as a group of three circular shafts in two tiers, united by an intermediate block and square plinth. The frieze was also card cut or pierced with intricate patterns, and cross stretchers were provided and similarly cut. Fret-cut brackets were frequently fixed between legs and frieze. Usually the top only is of solid wood; the gallery, frieze, stretchers, and probably the pierced leg faces will be found composed of layers of mahogany veneer alternating in direction of the grain, thus giving great strength. About 1765 the fret-cut gallery disappeared, together with the pierced construction, and very soon afterwards classical designs appeared in simple tables with square or turned taper legs.

By the middle of the century the tripod table was in great demand. The tripod foot (which varied but little) had the appearance of three inclined cabriole legs, which were dovetailed into the base of the central column. The latter was turned as a shaft or of baluster outline, and the best examples were carved not only on the stem but also on the three legs, and the feet cut into claw and ball, lion's paw, or dolphin heads. About 1755 an improvement was effected, whereby the top would not only revolve, in addition to being hinged, but by the with-drawal of a wedge could be lifted free of the tripod support. This was contrived by constructing a gallery which was hinged to the two cross-bearers on the under side of the top, and obtained a seating about the reduced apex of the central column and formed the bearing upon which the top could revolve. For the best work a single piece of mahogany was selected for the circular top, which was either sunk on the top surface, leaving a small raised mould at the edge, or the edge was cut and moulded in small balancing curves, known as a 'pie-crust' edge. Such tables were used for service of tea or supper. Mahogany specimens well turned on the stem, but entirely uncarved, were made continuously throughout the second half of the eighteenth century. In card tables the long cabriole legs provided an excellent field for carving over the knees, and up till about 1740 the lion mask was sometimes employed as decoration. The rounded corners of the top, with supporting cylinders in the frieze, continued until about 1750. The square angle breaking out from the straight or serpentine sides was introduced about 1740. With the adoption of the square leg the top became rectangular or serpentine, with the moulded edge often carved. Tables intended for dual use of card playing and tea had a couple of hinged flaps, the one felted and the other veneered. Plain, taper-turned legs with pad feet are to be found on some early mahogany card and tea tables. When closed, the table was of semi-circular form with two flaps, the first usually of solid mahogany to swing over, the second, also solid, was hinged on butts as a lid to the box formed within the under-framing. Three legs were permanently fixed to the semi-circular under-frame, two on the straight 'back' frame, and the third placed centrally on the curve; the fourth leg was mortised to a gate arm of the 'back' frame, pivoted on a wooden hinge to swing out and support the flap. In rare cases there were three flaps, when the top could be either of polished wood or felted.

Until about 1765-1770 (with the exception of the type just described) the extending legs were operated by elbow-jointed under framing, but with the general adoption of the circular top the two rear legs were attached each to a single arm of the under-frame. Some card tables were made in satinwood inlaid and painted. A fashionable shape for card tables was circular; this necessitated a semi-circular framing of pine, veneered either with mahogany or satinwood; the legs were inlaid where they crossed the frieze. The arrises of the legs and the top were inlaid with lines of box or holly, and the top flap was often inlaid with a large fan patera in which the light woods were shaded by scorching in hot sand. From about 1795 the tops were again straight-sided, but with boldly rounded corners without projections. The late taper legs were fitted with collars or stops about three inches up from the base.

The convenience of the two-flap arrangement of the gate-leg tables led to its revival in the form of the Pembroke table. These tables, which came in about 1765, were made in mahogany and satinwood. Some of the earliest had turned and fluted legs. Legs were also square tapered with line inlay, and about 1785

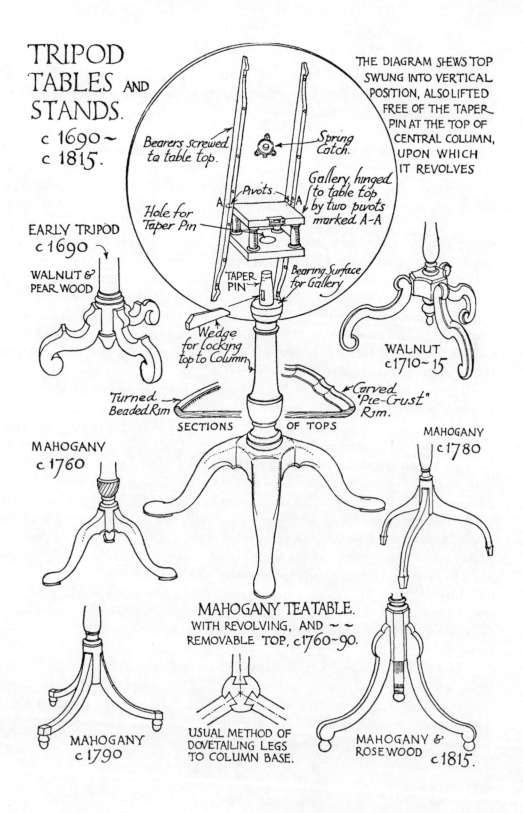

TRIPOD TABLES AND STANDS.

c 1690 ~ c 1815.

Bearers screwed to table top.

Spring Catch.

Pivots.

A A A A

Hole for Taper Pin

Gallery, hinged to table top by two pivots marked A-A

THE DIAGRAM SHEWS TOP SWUNG INTO VERTICAL POSITION, ALSO LIFTED FREE OF THE TAPER PIN AT THE TOP OF CENTRAL COLUMN, UPON WHICH IT REVOLVES

EARLY TRIPOD c 1690

WALNUT & PEAR WOOD

TAPER PIN

Bearing Surface for Gallery

Wedge for Locking top to Column

WALNUT c 1710 ~ 15

Turned Beaded Rim

SECTIONS OF TOPS

Carved "Pie-Crust" Rim.

MAHOGANY c 1760

MAHOGANY c 1780

MAHOGANY TEA TABLE.
WITH REVOLVING, AND ~ ~ REMOVABLE TOP, c 1760 ~ 90.

MAHOGANY c 1790

USUAL METHOD OF DOVETAILING LEGS TO COLUMN BASE.

MAHOGANY & ROSEWOOD c 1815.

were turned and moulded. The top was of thin wood and rectangular or oval in shape, the central fixed part being much larger in proportion to the flaps than earlier three-section table tops, owing to the flaps gaining support by one or two brackets (usually in beech) arranged to swing outward on wooden hinges. The flaps were hung on a pair of metal hinges, and closed on a rule joint. Many Pembroke tables were fitted with drawers at one end, lined in thin oak or mahogany, and running on bearer strips screwed to the side frames. At the opposite end it was usual to form dummy drawer fronts by fixing handles and inlaying border lines on the frieze. A large number of various small tables were made during the late eighteenth century usually resting on turned or taper legs and fitted with a drawer in the frieze. Occasionally the top was serpentine or bowed, and in some dating the legs are of the delicate French cabriole form, with carving on the flattish knee, which was swept in with a swell-shaped under frame.

Sofa tables were similar to Pembroke tables, but were of greater length. According to Sheraton's *Cabinet Dictionary* (1803) they measured between five to six feet in length. Many sofa tables have a sliding panel in the top, which can be reversed, the reverse being inlaid as a chess board.

Distinct from the bureau is the flat-topped library or pedestal table, which was usually designed to stand centrally in a room. This Georgian type of writing table is anticipated by an example of oak made for Samuel Pepys and preserved in the Pepysian Library at Magdalene College, Cambridge. There is a wide lacuna between this table, and two pedestal tables designed by William Kent for Lord Burlington about 1735. In one of these the knee-hole is framed in a flattened arch, and the large carved enrichments are gilt; in the second table, which is five sided, the angles are faced with carved and gilt owl-headed terminals which finish in claw and ball feet. There is little change in the structure of pedestal library tables during the course of the eighteenth century; but the mouldings are reduced in size and massive angle terminals are rarely introduced.

Lighter forms of writing tables are figured in Sheraton's works, and care was bestowed on the writer's convenience. Among these the best known is the Carlton House table, a design for which appears in 1796 in Gillow's cost books.

This design also appears in Sheraton's *Drawing Book* in a plate dated 1791 and described as a 'Lady's Drawing and writing table'. It unites a large writing space with accessible accommodation in the low superimposed top, which is fitted with drawers. A characteristic feature is the curved plane descending from the upper tier of drawers to the lower.

Early in the nineteenth century a writing table form was introduced, supported on a turned column with curved legs. The top was usually drum-shaped, with the frieze filled with drawers.

Bedroom furniture was seldom of mahogany before 1735 and the small walnut four-legged table, or the knee-hole table with drawers, served as a stand for the mirror.

Mahogany chests of drawers, often with knee recess, were used for the toilet, and in these the top drawer was specially fitted with a collapsible mirror on a ratchet. During the last quarter of the eighteenth century many fine dressing tables were designed to appear like a commode or writing table. A mirror operated by a spring dropped into a slide at the back of the top. They were made in inlaid mahogany or satinwood and in painted pine. Apart from these fashionable pieces, the mahogany dressing chest remained in favour, and upon which stood the separate mirror.

Illustrations on pages 212, 217, 218, 227-233, 237 and 239.

XI

THE CLOTHES PRESS AND WARDROBE

THE clothes press, consisting of a cupboard fitted with sliding shelves mounted upon a chest of drawers, was the usual receptacle for clothes in the reign of George III and hanging wardrobes sometimes made with doors the full height were not general until the last quarter of the century. Some wardrobes dating about 1740-1760 had the panels flush with the framing, often finely veneered and bordered with applied wavy mouldings with gaps at the corners where leaf carving was applied. The cornice was frequently surmounted by a fret-cut cresting.

Large wardrobes dating from about 1750 were constructed with a break front in three sections, the centre part being formed as a clothes press on a chest of drawers, the wings being arranged as hanging cupboards with long doors. Examples of this arrangement are figured in Sheraton's *Drawing Book* (1791-4) and described in the text as containing six or seven clothes press shelves in the upper middle part and wings filled with 'arms' and coat hangers. From about this date the cornice was pedimented or straight, with cresting omitted; the raised panel moulds became straight and were either mitred at the corners or connected with short concave quadrants of the same section (usually astragal), on the outer sides of which a carved or turned rosette was often applied.

Wardrobes of average quality made during the last quarter of the eighteenth century were mostly of 'batchelor' type, in two parts. The top half had sides of solid mahogany, dovetailed to the top and bottom of pine: the panelled pine back was screwed into rebates. The cornice was generally a separate unit, framed in pine and faced with mahogany mouldings, with, in some cases, a cross-banded veneered frieze. The pair of doors were often framed and panelled in Cuba wood, the panels being veneered on the outer face with curl figure and surrounded by a tiny moulding in the rebate.

To cover the joint between the meeting stiles an astragal moulded brass strip was screwed to the locking door. The interior was fitted with sliding oak trays.

The bottom half was generally constructed of pine, veneered with straight grained mahogany at the sides, and with curl on the front. The drawers (usually four) have oak linings and mahogany cock beading around the edges. Around the top edge a moulding was fixed to hide the junction with the top half of the wardrobe. The base was either a moulded plinth with bracket feet or the French swept foot. In early nineteenth century specimens squat turned stumps supported the wardrobe, which became impoverished in the design.

Illustration on page 219.

XII

SIDEBOARDS

THE sideboard proper, as distinct from the side table, was a product of the reign of George III. The designs of Robert Adam are the first in which the pedestal and central table are shown, and examples designed by him still exist at Kedleston, Harewood House and Saltram. The central table was often fitted with a brass gallery for the support of plates; the pedestals which served as cellarets or plate-warmers were surmounted by urns (either of wood or metal).

The gradual changes in form and arrangement may be outlined as follows:

1 The first type consisted of a side table, with the addition of flanking detached pedestals supporting urns of mahogany, lined with lead and fitted with draincocks.

2 The flanking pedestals became connected to the board. The urns were fitted as knife boxes with slots for knives, forks, and spoons. Owing to the difficulty of hinging a circular lid, a central tube was provided with an inner lining to which the lid was secured, and by which it could be raised to get at the contents. Later, the shape became octagonal. Drawers were fitted in the frieze and also in the pedestals.

3 About 1770 the pedestals began to be modified, the supports of the sideboard being turned or taper legs arranged in threes or fours at each end (two in front and one or two at the back). The legs became shorter as the body became higher in proportion. A lower drawer or cupboard was often fitted between the end pair of legs, the central bay being usually open below the frieze drawer to allow space for the standing wine cooler.

From 1770 the front was generally shaped, the favourite form being a flattish bow or a serpentine curve with a concave centre with convex flanking curves, or *vice versa*. This necessitated the shaping of cupboard and drawer fronts to agree with the curves of the framing. Drawers were lined with fine quality, thin, figured oak or Honduras mahogany. Small sideboards were designed without a

DEVELOPMENT OF THE SIDEBOARD c1760 ~ c1805.

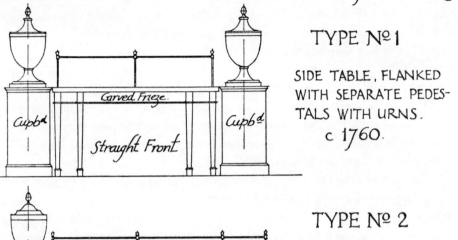

TYPE Nº 1

SIDE TABLE, FLANKED
WITH SEPARATE PEDES-
TALS WITH URNS.
c 1760.

Carved Frieze.

Cupbᵈ

Cupbᵈ

Straight Front

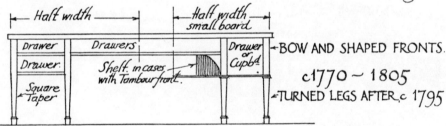

TYPE Nº 2

DESIGNED AS A COMPLETE
UNIT, WITH AND WITH~
OUT URNS AND RAIL:

c 1765.

Drawers or Carved Frieze.

Drawers or Cupbᵈs

Drawers or Cupbᵈs

Straight & Shaped Fronts.

TYPE Nº 3.

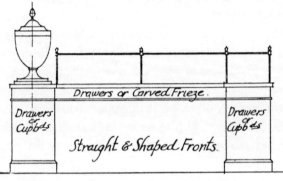

— Half width —

— Half width small board —

Drawer

Drawer.

Drawers

Drawer or Cupbᵈ

←BOW AND SHAPED FRONTS.

c1770 ~ 1805

←TURNED LEGS AFTER c 1795

Shelf. in cases with Tambour front.

Square Taper

TYPE Nº 4

RETURN TO EARLIER.
PEDESTAL TYPE, BUT
HEAVIER IN DESIGN.

c 1805.

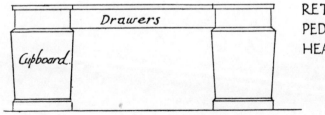

Drawers

Cupboard.

definite frieze; they had a centre shallow drawer with a single square cupboard or deep drawer at each side. These small specimens seldom can be dated prior to 1780. The space beneath the central drawer was usually (though not always) arched at the corners by brackets and when not entirely open was fitted with a shelf, which was occasionally enclosed with a tambour front after 1785.

A brass rail raised about twelve inches on turned brass supports was often fitted at the back. The decoration of the early sideboards was very restrained: the frieze was fluted and carved. It is unusual to find sideboards entirely of satinwood before the late years of the eighteenth century.

The edges of the top were usually square and were often cross-banded.

A large semi-circular recess at the ends of rooms was frequently planned in the dining-room to receive the sideboard; and in such cases this was designed to fit the curve. Variety and interest were obtained by treating the front with convex and concave curves, producing a gradation of tone on the finely figured panels. With the exception of the legs, the carcase construction was in seasoned deal or pine and the drawer fronts of mahogany, often built up, upon which the veneers and inlays were glued down. Borders were frequently cross-banded and joined on the mitre. With the Regency period sideboards returned to the solid pedestal type and became massive.

Illustrations on pages 234 and 235.

XIII

BEDS

WITH the use of mahogany the covered bedstead was no longer in fashion; and during the reign of George II the wooden structure was exposed. The posts at the foot were turned and carved in low relief above the level of the mattress; at the base they terminated in short cabriole legs; but about 1750 these were omitted and a small plinth was added to the square post. The head posts were plain square tapered, intended to be hidden by curtains; generally they were in a native hard wood. The carved cornice appeared either with or without a covering of material. At the junction of the valances the projecting holders of the *cantonnières* were usually of scroll form. Beds in the Chinese taste were decorated in that style and were surmounted by hoods and canopies resembling pagoda roofs. About 1760 the foot posts became still more delicate and were generally fluted on the taper above a vase form. In some instances low relief carving appeared in sunk panels on the square lower portions of the foot posts, which began to taper to a spade plinth.

During the classical revival some few state beds were designed enriched with gilding. During the last quarter of the century beds were marked by graceful proportions and refinement of detail; the posts were turned, reeded and carved with the water-leaf, palm-leaf and wheat-ear. The cornice was frequently bowed or serpentine, carved, pierced and inlaid. Painted decoration is to be found on some examples.

In early years of the nineteenth century, decadence in the design becomes apparent; and the foot posts lost their proportions. During the Regency designers followed the French fashion for beds with low head and footboards which sometimes curved outwards.

In beds dating from the eighteenth and early nineteenth century the side and end beams were tenoned into the four posts and secured with coach screws. The sinkings for the screws were covered up round an oval brass disc, with a screw lug or an eye on the edge. A series of wooden laths replaced the earlier roped-on canvas mattress. The turning of the long posts was an expensive and difficult undertaking on the lathe and although it is usually impossible to detect the joint, many posts were built up of two parts and united by a strong dowel; this economised material and enabled the turning to be done on a lathe of normal size, as only the best-equipped workshops could boast of a lathe capable of receiving a post about eight feet long.

Illustrations on pages 220 and 221.

XIV

STANDS

Portable stands were used to supplement the light given by wall lights and chandeliers to afford 'additional light to such parts of the room where it would be neither ornamental nor easy to introduce any other kind'. In the early Georgian period gilt wood and parcel-gilt stands were designed under the influence of the Palladian architects in the form of terms. Other stands often have shafts of baluster form finishing in a vase immediately underneath the tray. In the *Director* the tripod form is shown as the base of several designs for candlestands in mahogany and japanned wood; and in surviving examples of the rococo period the shaft is sometimes built up in an elaborate fashion, the centre being flanked by scrollwork and other devices. In the late Georgian period, elements from classical models were combined in novel forms. A favourite type consisted of three slender curved uprights supporting the top and enclosing a central column or vase.

The whatnot, an open stand fitted with tiers of shelves one above another for keeping and displaying various objects, such as ornaments, curiosities, papers, appears in the late years of the eighteenth and early nineteenth centuries. In some cases the top is fitted with a marble slab and the feet with castors.

Stands designed to hold plates and cutlery were used in the dining-room where service was dispensed with. These canterburies 'made to stand by a table at supper, with a circular end and three partitions cross-wise, to hold knives, forks, plates', are illustrated in Sheraton's *Cabinet Dictionary* (1803). In the upper portion the circular end is sometimes surrounded by a gallery. Stands constructed to contain bound volumes of music also contained partitions, and were 'adapted to run in under a pianoforte'.

The dumb waiter, which is structurally an upright pole bearing trays of graduated size, and resting on a tripod base, appears among advertisements and accounts during the reign of George I. Its tripod base ensured stability and its trays were sometimes bordered with a rim to prevent the bottles and glasses from falling off them. In the late years of the eighteenth century new varieties were introduced having a four-legged base and greater accommodation on the upper portion. During the Regency period the dumb waiter of pole and tray type is characterized by increased solidity.

Illustrations on pages 236 and 239.

EF—K

XV

LONG-CASE CLOCKS

URING the reigns of the first two Georges the cases of long clocks were either japanned or veneered with walnut, and continued to be so veneered until figured mahogany was imported. The tall and slender proportion which characterized the clocks of William III and Anne's reigns was seldom repeated; the mahogany cases were wider, the body shorter, and the base was usually somewhat squat. The hood was arched and surmounted by shaped crestings or a pediment with finials. The hood door will be found hinged on a pair of projecting butts, so that it opens within the angle columns, the latter being permanently fixed. The body door was headed by a shouldered arch and prior to about 1760 a raised panel was generally placed on the base. The carcase was of oak, mahogany or pine, veneered with figured mahogany or japanned. Fine specimens in mahogany had applied frets on the splayed corners and on the frieze. Carving was also present on the hood, the case door and the plinth.

A large number of country clock cases were made during the second half of the eighteenth century in oak, at times inlaid on the solid. A number of them were only thirty-hour clocks and had painted iron dials. For cheapness they retained the straight cornice with the square head to the dial and case door. There is a considerable difference between the long-case clocks of Scotland and the Northern Counties of England (Lancashire, Cheshire and Yorkshire) during the late eighteenth and early nineteenth centuries. The northern cases are broader in proportion to their height and in some examples there is a good deal of applied fretwork and carved enrichment. Two examples from Lancashire, in the Victoria and Albert Museum dating from the late years of the eighteenth century, show the characteristic girth, the high base and scrolled pediments.[1]

Early in the nineteenth century the long-case clock is described by Sheraton as 'almost obsolete in London',[2] but he proposed to give designs of them in his *Cabinet Maker's, Upholsterers and General Artist's Encyclopaedia*, 'to serve his country friends'.

Illustrations on page 226.

---

[1] Long-case clock by Barker, Wigan (*circa* 1785), long-case clock by Edward Shepley, Manchester, (*circa* 1790).

[2] *Cabinet Dictionary* (1803). Only the first volume of the encyclopaedia was published (1805).

XVI

WASHSTANDS

IT was not until the mid-Georgian period that a specialized piece of furniture designed as a washing stand appears. Many designs are figured in the third edition of the *Director* (1762), the *Guide* (1788), the *Drawing Book* (1791-94) and the *Cabinet Dictionary* (1803). In several instances washing stands were disguised to look like a cabinet or chest of drawers, in order that 'they may stand in a genteel room, without giving offence to the eye'.[1] An early type was a small stand, which was composed of three or four uprights, shaped and turned and connected at the top by a circular moulded rim to take a small bowl; half-way down, the legs were framed in with a square or triangular drawer, upon which stood a spherical soap box. At the base a triangular or square block was supported by three or four spreading feet of cabriole form. Other forms were variations of a small cabinet upon legs with top and front hinged to open, the interior being fitted and including a sliding mirror at the back.

A simple and well-known type, dating from about 1770, was the bow-fronted corner washstand, supported upon three rectangular legs, the top holed centrally for a basin and at each side for turned wooden cups. The back was formed of two boards of shaped outline meeting in the angle. Beneath the top a cupboard with a pair of doors was arranged, or instead and more usually, a shelf connected the legs half-way down with a shallow drawer fitted beneath; also, to tie in the slender legs a second shelf with concave edges was fitted a few inches above the floor. Inlay provided the decoration on fine veneered specimens. Those made of pine, finished and decorated with painting, can seldom be dated prior to 1785.

Illustration on page 233.

---

[1] Sheraton, *Cabinet Dictionary*, 1803.

XVII

MIRRORS AND DRESSING GLASSES

THE changes in form of mirrors during the Georgian period were remarkably rapid. During the early Georgian period the mirror gave a rich opportunity for architectural treatment. The component parts were a moulded architrave forming the frame and a frieze and cornice surmounted by a pediment; the architrave terminated in base scrolls and rested upon a surbase mould, beneath which a shaped apron piece was fixed, ornamented with carving. These frames were chiefly of gilt pinewood; others were faced with mahogany or walnut enriched with gilt mouldings and carving. Gesso also played an important part in decorating the gilt specimens and was still popular as the chief means of working the enrichment on the less important mirror frames.

A mirror of distinctive form was the chimney glass, a long glass to stand on the mantelshelf. The frame, which was about one and a half to two inches wide, was overlaid with walnut or gilt gesso. In certain cases the short sides were enriched with projecting scroll-pieces carved with acanthus. The mirror was arranged in three bevelled plates, a long centre with a narrow plate on each side, the former just clipping the side bevels of the latter.

In mirrors for great houses the rococo found its freest and most capricious expression. The period of free rococo design passed through various phases between about 1740 and 1765. In the early stage, the blend of French *rocaille* and certain Chinese details is freely exploited in the *Director* (1754), and in the work of contemporary designers. Later, the basis of the designs is a system of graceful and sinuous scrolls, incorporating some floral details. In the full rococo period, nothing that could be balanced into a symmetry was left symmetrical. The carving of frames was a specialized industry and it is stated in the *London Tradesman* (1747) that there was 'a class of carvers who do nothing else but carve frames for looking-glasses'. The ornament was carefully finished in frames between about 1745 and 1760 and the surface was not overloaded with a preparation of size and whiting before gilding. After 1760 the practice of heavily preparing the ground was again resumed. In mirrors of this period the plate was no longer bevelled.

During the classical revival frames of large glasses were usually rectangular. Small oval and rectangular mirrors were framed in a narrow moulding surmounted by a cresting of open design. These open enrichments were usually moulded in composition and threaded on wire cores. A type of mahogany-framed mirror which became popular about the middle of the eighteenth century was composed on the lines of the narrow walnut frames. It was a tall rectangle with a small inward point at the two top corners, to which the bevelled edge of the plate was made to correspond; and a projecting flat outer frame, or surround, narrow at the sides, but widening at the top and base with fret-cut edges. The top cresting was generally enriched with a gilt bird, carved in relief in a pierced circle. The edge of the frame against the glass had a gilt fillet. An innovation of the late eighteenth century was the convex mirror, which is figured in Ince and Mayhew's *Household Furniture*. This mirror was enclosed in a moulded circular gilt frame, the outer edge reeded and banded at intervals with cross-ribbons, and with a black reeded fillet next the glass; in the hollow of the moulding small gilt balls were applied at intervals. Such mirrors were often surmounted by an eagle with outspread wings or with carved foliage.

Contemporary with the circular convex mirror was a type of rectangular overmantel glass, designed usually with bevelled central and two side plates, surrounded and separated by a narrow reeded frame; a bold pilaster stood at each side, the whole being crowned with hollow moulded cornice in which the row of balls also appears. Square bosses were generally arranged at the junctions of the framing, faced with paterae; feet were provided of spherical form. Such mirrors were popular throughout the first third of the nineteenth century and to the end of it in country districts.

Little mirrors mounted upon box stands containing drawers continued in favour for many years as dressing glasses. Prior to 1735-1740 mahogany toilet mirrors were a rarity and were not common before 1750. The early models were designed with a rectangular mirror in a narrow moulded frame, having an inward point at the two top corners and an inner carved and gilt fillet. This frame was suspended by brass screw mirror movements on square tapered uprights, usually moulded and fitted with turned finials. The base was a shallow veneered box containing one row of small drawers and was supported on bracket feet under a small plinth mould. The faces of the drawers and framing were shaped concave in section, with usually a small ovolo around the top edges. In many cases a fret-cut cresting was fitted to the mirror-head, but is seldom intact to-day. The glass plate was finished with a wide bevel. During the reign of George III the shield and oval form was introduced. To fit to the shaped sides of these mirrors, the slender uprights were also curved at the lower end. The stand contained a row of small drawers, often bowed or serpentine. The mirror frame was very narrow, quite flat and cross-banded. The shield-shape was built up of sections of pine; the oval was constructed by wrapping a narrow strip of yew or other easily bendable wood around a former until the desired width was obtained. The box and drawer faces were veneered and in many cases the mirror supports also. Arris lines and borders of lighter woods and ebony were applied; ivory or bone was used for urn finials or rosettes on the uprights and as pulls and escutcheons on the drawers. The carcase or box of the stand was invariably framed in pine, the drawer linings being of very thin oak or mahogany. Mirrors of this type were also veneered with satinwood.

When the box stand with drawers was omitted, mirrors were known as cheval glasses. The oval mirror was sometimes arranged with the major axis horizontal and suspended in a frame consisting of uprights, framed into trestle feet and connected by a shaped stretcher. On this framing a border line was incised or a holly line inlaid.

The less expensive mirrors had rectangular frames and this form became popular from about 1800, when the uprights (and stretchers when no stand was fitted) were turned in very refined and delicate profiles. The face of the mirror frame was still cross-banded and was frequently of convex section. The mirror movements were often faced with turned knobs.

Illustrations on pages 222-225.

XVIII

FIRE SCREENS

Existing fire screens are of two forms. The horse (or cheval) screen consisted of a rectangular frame with a shaped top flanked by two posts, which carried down to trestle feet, connected by turned or carved stretchers. An early example of the horse fire screen is the gilt carved screen at Hampton Court Palace dating from the reign of William III. In this the baluster uprights are supported by scrolled bases and the cresting is pierced and carved in the French taste. Horse fire screens are illustrated both in the *Director* (1754) and the *Guide* (1788). In the latter work, a sliding panel for a screen 'intended to slide up out of the pillars that are on each side' is figured on one plate.

In the lighter pole screen which became popular in the middle years of the eighteenth century, the framed panel was arranged to slide on a slender pole and to be secured at any height by means of a spring or screw. The base took the form of a tripod; the panel frame was at first rectangular and often carved with the flower and ribbon. From early in George III's reign panels assumed shield, oval and rectangular shapes. Examples dating from the last years of the nineteenth century often had a solid turned or shaped base instead of the tripod foot. Both pole and horse fire screens were mounted with panels of needlework, prints, water-colour drawings and Chinese paper.

Illustrations on page 240.

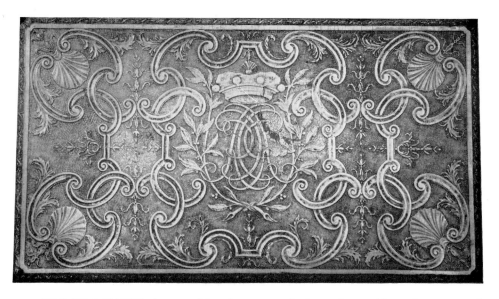

115. TOP OF A TABLE, decorated in gilt gesso with the cypher and baron's coronet of Richard Temple, Lord Cobham. (Formerly at Stowe House, Buckinghamshire.) (By James Moore.) *c. 1715.*

116. SIDE TABLE, decorated in the frieze and upper part of the legs with gilt gesso. *c. 1715.* From Chicheley Hall, Buckinghamshire.

118. CORNER CHAIR, with drop-in seat, the front leg carved.
c. 1740. From Colonel L. and Mrs. Jenner.
Height, 2 ft 8 ins

117. CORNER CHAIR, with drop-in seat, the splats pierced.
Mid-eighteenth century. From Colonel L. and Mrs. Jenner.
Height, 3 ft 9 ins

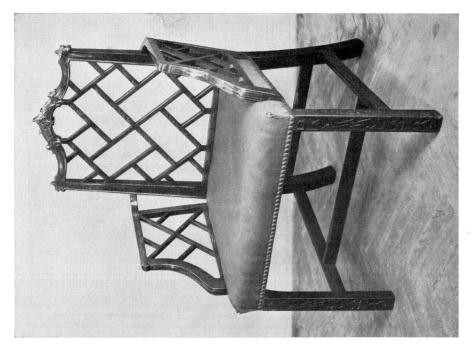

120. ARMCHAIR, the back and arms filled in with lattice-work. *c.* 1760. From Mr. Frank Partridge.

119. ARMCHAIR, the splat filled in with lattice-work. *c.* 1760. From Lady Wilson-Todd, Halnaby Hall, Yorkshire.

Height, 3 ft   *Width,* 2 ft 2¾ ins

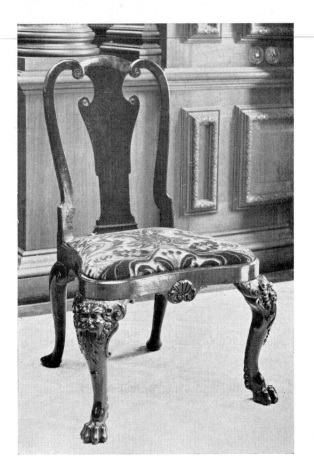

121. WALNUT CHAIR, with solid splat and feet carved with a lion mask. *c.* 1735. From the Viscount Leverhulme Collection.

Height, 3 ft 4 ins

122. CHAIR, with pierced splat and legs carved with a lion mask and finishing in paw feet. *c.* 1740. From the S. B. Joel Collection.

123. ARMCHAIR, the splat pierced in the Gothic taste. Mid-eighteenth century. From Stourhead, Wiltshire.

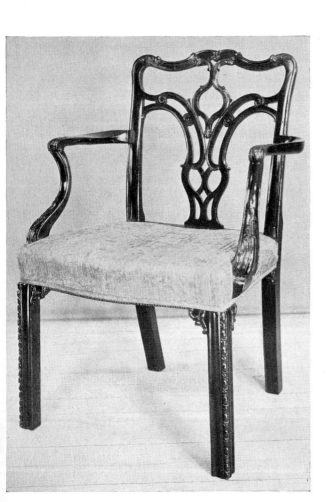

124. ARMCHAIR, with pierced splat connected to the back uprights. c. 1760.

Ladder and wheel back chairs

125. SINGLE CHAIR (ladder back), the legs connected by a stretcher. c. 1770. From the Stephen Winkworth Collection.

> Height, 3 ft 1 in
> Width, 1 ft 11 ins

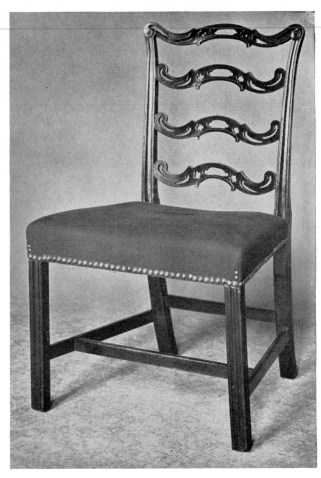

126. SINGLE CHAIR (wheel back), the legs connected by a cross-stretcher. c. 1780. From the Viscount Northampton, Castle Ashby, Northamptonshire.

127. ARMCHAIR, the framework painted, the seat caned. Late eighteenth century. From Ston Easton, Somerset.

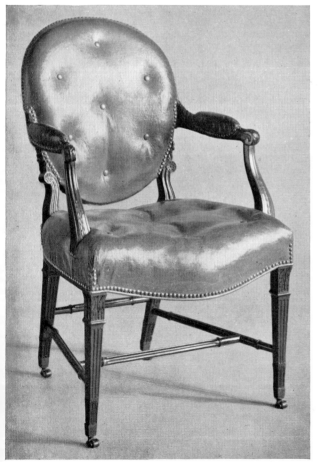

128. ARMCHAIR, the tapered and fluted legs connected by stretchers. The back and seat covered with the original red leather. *c.* 1780. From Sir John Ramsden, Bulstrode Park, Buckinghamshire.

Height, 3 ft   *Width,* 1 ft 10½ ins

129. ARMCHAIR, painted, back and seat caned, late eighteenth century. From Ston Easton, Somerset.

130. SINGLE CHAIR, with panelled top rail and splat formed as a classic tripod. *c.* 1790. From Mr. J. F. Roxburgh.

131. ARMCHAIR, of solid satinwood, inlaid with ebony stringing. (Made by Thomas Chippendale, junior.) 1802. From Stourhead, Wiltshire.

132. SINGLE CHAIR, the framework and panel in the back painted. *c.* 1790. From the Earl of Yarborough, Brocklesby, Lincolnshire. *Height*, 2 ft 9 ins

133. STOOL, of oval plan, with drop-in seat and legs finishing in lion-paw feet. *c.* 1740.

134. STOOL, with pierced stretchers. *c.* 1760. From Lord Methuen, Corsham Court, Wiltshire.

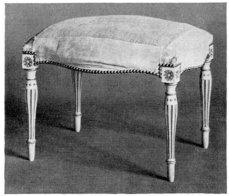

135. STOOL, painted, with gilt details (part of a set). *c.* 1775. From Blickling Hall, Norfolk. *Height*, 1 ft 6½ ins *Width*, 1 ft 10 ins

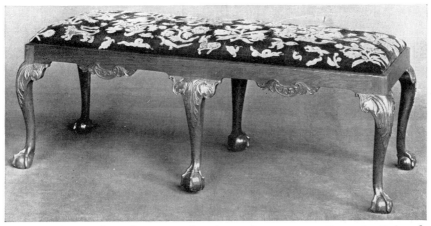

136. STOOL, with six legs, carved with acanthus. *c.* 1735. From the Duke of Devonshire, Hardwick Hall, Derbyshire. *Height*, 1 ft 8½ ins *Length*, 4 ft 4½ ins

137. SETTEE, the legs carved with a shell and husk pendant, and finishing in claw and ball feet. *c.* 1730. From Ripley Castle, Yorkshire.

    Height, 3 ft 1½ ins   *Width*, 4 ft

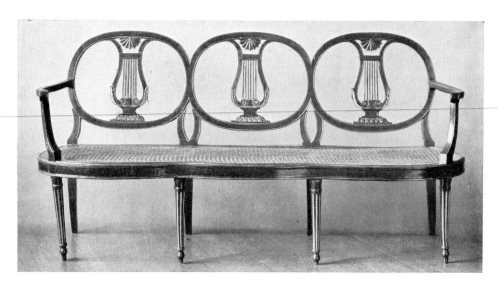

138. SETTEE, painted, with gilt details, the seat caned. *c.* 1785. From the Earl of Sandwich, Hinchingbrooke, Huntingdonshire.

    Height, 3 ft 1½ ins   *Width*, 6 ft 3½ ins

139. SETTEE, painted, last years of eighteenth century. From Ston Easton, Somerset.

140. SOFA, of beech grained in imitation of rosewood, the feet mounted with ormolu shoes and casters. *c.* 1810. From Mr. Norman Adams.

Height (of seat), 1 ft 6 ins   *Length*, 5 ft 3 ins

141. KNEE-HOLE LIBRARY TABLE, with carved mouldings. *c.* 1735. From the Earl of Yarborough, Brocklesby, Lincolnshire.

Height, 2 ft 6 ins   *Width*, 4 ft 8½ ins

142. LIBRARY TABLE, with a hinged flap (one of a pair which, placed together, form one large table). *c.* 1760. From Mr. Frank Partridge.   *Height*, 3 ft   *Width*, 5 ft 6 ins

144. DAVENPORT, fitted with a desk that slides forward. c. 1800.

143. BUREAU, with tambour front enclosing the desk portion. c. 1800. From Colonel L. and Mrs. Jenner.

Height, 3 ft 6 ins   *Width*, 3 ft 1½ ins

Bookcases

145. BOOKCASE, break-fronted, the central section surmounted by an open pediment. c. 1745. From the James Thursby-Pelham Collection.

Height, 6 ft 6 ins
Length, 5 ft

146. BOOKCASE, the glazed upper stage surmounted by a fretted swan-necked pediment. Late eighteenth century. From the India Office.

Height, 9 ft 5 ins   *Width*, 4 ft 7 ins

148. BOOKCASE of pine, break-fronted, the central section sur-mounted by an open pediment. *c.* 1780.

147. BOOKCASE, break-fronted, the central section sur-mounted by an open pediment, the drawers and plinth enriched with frets. *c.* 1765. From Mr. C. D. Rotch.

Height, 8 ft 5 ins   *Length,* 7 ft 4 ins

149. DWARF BOOKCASE, with interior shelves concealed by an exterior swinging case of shelves. Early years of the nineteenth century. From the late William Ranken.

150. BOOKCASE (of maple, inlaid with ebony), the marble top bordered by a brass gallery. *c.* 1800. From the Earl of Shaftesbury, St. Giles's House, Dorset.

151. BOOKCASE, inlaid and cross-banded, the cupboard doors fitted with a brass wire trellis. Last years of the eighteenth century. From Burford House, Shropshire.

> *Height*, 9 ft 2 ins
> *Length*, 5 ft 5 ins

152. CABINET, on table stand, veneered with zebrawood. *c.* 1790. From the late Sir A. Richardson, Avenue House, Ampthill, Bedfordshire.

> *Height*, 3 ft 7 ins   *Width*, 3 ft

Bookcase and writing table

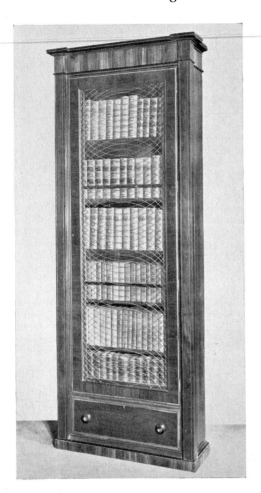

153. BOOKCASE (one of a pair), fitted with a drawer in the base, the door fitted with a brass wire trellis. *c.* 1795. From Mr. L. Knight.

> *Height,* 7 ft 6 ins
> *Width,* 2 ft

154. WRITING TABLE, of satinwood veneer, cross-banded and painted with flowers. *c.* 1785. From the Earl of Bradford, Weston Park, Staffordshire.

> *Height,* 3 ft 8 ins
> *Width,* 3 ft 1 in

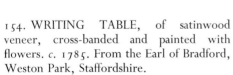

155. DOUBLE CHEST of DRAWERS (tallboy), the frieze and canted corners enriched with frets. *c.* 1760. From Captain Frank Gilbey.

156. WARDROBE, veneered with satinwood, the upper stage surmounted by a 'Greek' pediment, and antefixae. *c.* 1815. From the Mansion House, London.

157. BED, with panelled head board and carved frieze and cornice. The posts (of cluster-column form) finish in claw and ball feet. *c.* 1740. From Charlecote Park, Warwickshire.

158. BED, with mahogany posts and painted frieze and cornice. *c.* 1780. From Howsham Hall, Yorkshire.

159. CHIMNEY GLASS, composed of three plates, surmounted by painting of the Grand Canal, Venice. The frame carved with palm branches and rococo ornament. Mid-eighteenth century.

160. CHIMNEY GLASS, composed of three plates, surmounted by a painting. The carved and parcel-gilt frame is surmounted by an openwork cresting. *c.* 1730. From Sezincote, Gloucestershire.

161. MIRROR, the central bevelled plate surrounded by shaped and bevelled sections, framed in a gilt gesso moulding, and surmounted by a pierced cresting. *c. 1720.* From Sir John Carew Pole, Bart., Antony House, Cornwall.

Height, 5 ft 5 ins

162. MIRROR, oval, surrounded by a carved and gilt moulding, and by sections of mirror glass overlaid with gilt detail. *c. 1765.* From Sir John Carew Pole, Bart., Antony House, Cornwall.

Height, 4 ft 5 ins

163. Mirror, oval, in a carved and gilt frame. Mid-eighteenth century. From Rufford Hall, Lancashire.

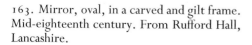

166. OBLONG MIRROR, framed in moulded, carved and gilt frame, and surmounted by light open-work cresting and pendant. *c.* 1780. From Bank House, Wisbech.

165. CONVEX MIRROR, contained in a reeded ebonized border and gilt surround set with balls. The finial is an eagle displayed. *c.* 1810. From the Victoria and Albert Museum.

Height, 3 ft 7¾ ins
Diameter of frame, 2 ft 1¾ ins

164. MIRROR, oval, in a carved and gilt frame surmounted by a cresting consisting of a medallion framed in trails of foliage. *c.* 1770. From Ham House, Surrey.

167. DRESSING GLASS, on stand fitted with three drawers, the uprights reeded. *c.* 1795.

> *Height,* 2 ft 11 ins
> *Width,* 3 ft 2¾ ins

168. DRESSING GLASS, on serpentine-fronted stand fitted with three drawers, the plate bordered by a gesso moulding. *c.* 1760. From the Cecil Higgins Collection.

> *Height,* 2 ft 3½ ins
> *Width,* 1 ft 9 ins

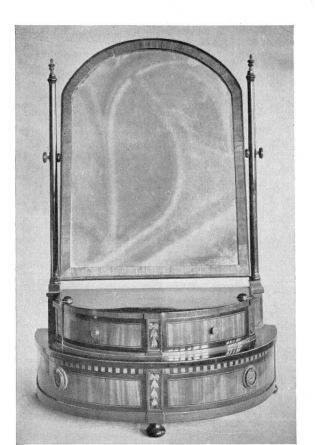

169. DRESSING GLASS, on semi-elliptical stand inlaid. *c.* 1785.

> *Height,* 2 ft 3½ ins   *Width,* 1 ft 6¼ ins

170. ACT OF PARLIAMENT
CLOCK, with large dial and short
trunk. *c.* 1740. From the India Office.

171. (*left*). LONG-CASE CLOCK
(the movement by Davison, Eccles-
ham). The wide hood surmounted by
a pediment and finials. The trunk
flanked with quarter corinthian columns on a vertical base. *c.* 1765.
From the Victoria and Albert
Museum.

Height, 7 ft 11½ ins

172. (*right*). LONG-CASE CLOCK
(the movement by Standring, Bolton).
The large hood is surmounted by an
open pediment, the spandrels beneath
are painted with arabesques on glass.
The trunk flanked by Ionic quarter
columns on a bricked base. From the
Lady Lever Art Gallery, Port Sunlight. *c.* 1760.

Height, 8 ft 2 ins

173. CONSOLE TABLE, with marble top, the carved and gilt support an eagle displayed. *c.* 1730. From the Lady Capel Cure Collection.

174. CONSOLE TABLE, with marble top, the two dolphins, carved and gilt, form the support. *c.* 1730. From the Duke of Buccleuch, Boughton House, Northamptonshire.

Height, 2 ft $7\frac{3}{4}$ ins   *Width,* 3 ft $4\frac{1}{2}$ ins

175. SIDE TABLE, with marble top, the frieze carved with the Vitruvian scroll, the cabriole legs finishing in claw and ball feet. *c. 1725*. From Hardwick Hall, Shropshire.

176. SIDE TABLE, with marble top, the legs carved with a lion mask and finishing in paw feet, the apron carved with drapery swags centring in a female mask. From Ripley Castle, Yorkshire.

Height, 2 ft 8 ins *Width*, 4 ft 3 ins

177. CARD TABLE, with shaped and fluted frieze. *c.* 1780.
From Mr. Leonard Knight.

      Height, 2 ft 6 ins   *Width*, 3 ft

178. SIDE TABLE, inlaid on the top with musical instruments, and on the
frieze and legs with husks. *c.* 1780. From the George Donaldson Collection.

      Height, 2 ft 11 ins   *Length*, 4 ft 8 ins

179. DROP-LEAF TABLE (one of a pair), the frieze fluted and the legs carved with a water leaf. *c.* 1780. From the Frederick Behrens Collection.

Height, 2 ft 5 ins

180. DROP-LEAF TABLE, of kingwood, cross-banded with tulipwood. (The top when lifted discloses a well.) From Mr. Norman Adams.

Height, 2 ft 4½ ins

181. SIDE TABLE, with top and shelf of white marble. From Trinity House, London. Early years of the nineteenth century.

182. SIDE TABLE, with carved terminal supports, the frieze and terms mounted with gilt brass enrichments. *c.* 1800. From the Earl of Bradford, Weston Park, Staffordshire.

Height, 2 ft 11 ins
Length, 4 ft 3½ ins

183. DINING TABLE, oval, with two flaps, supported on carved legs finishing in lion paw feet. *c.* 1740. From Crowcombe Court, Somerset.

Height, 2 ft 4¾ ins   Length, 5 ft 7½ ins

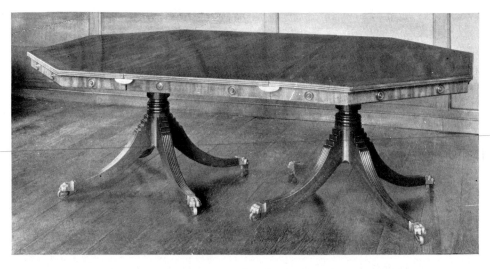

184. DINING TABLE, on two pedestals. From Mrs. F. Lycett Green.

185. TRIPOD TABLE, with pierced and carved gallery, carved shaft and legs. *c.* 1750. From the Lady Lever Art Gallery, Port Sunlight, Cheshire.

Width across, 2 ft 7½ ins

186. WASHSTAND, with the top enclosed by flaps supported on brackets. *c.* 1770. From Hardwick Hall, Derbyshire.

Height, 2 ft 8½ ins
Length (open), 3 ft 2 ins
Depth, 1 ft 6 ins

187. SIDEBOARD, serpentine-fronted, and inlaid with a shell on the apron below the central drawer. *c.* 1780.

188. SIDEBOARD, with fluted, tapered feet. From Denton Hall, Yorkshire.

189. SIDEBOARD TABLE, resting on reeded legs, finishing in lion paw feet. From the Bedford Hotel, Brighton. *c.* 1810.

Height, 3 ft 1 in   *Length*, 7 ft 6 ins

190. SIDEBOARD (one of a pair), made for an angle. *c.* 1790. From Earl Spencer, Althorp, Northamptonshire.

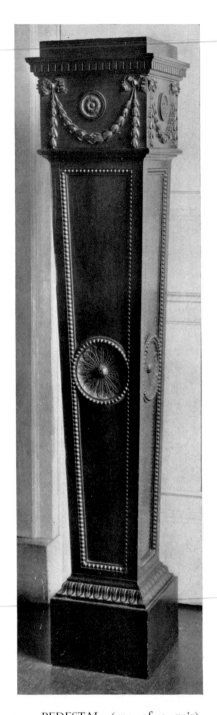

192. TRIPOD STAND. From Mr. Leonard Knight.
Height, 2 ft 10 ins

191. PEDESTAL (one of a pair),
supporting a candelabrum. *c. 1775*.
From Padworth House, Berkshire.
   Height, 4 ft 6 ins

193. DRESSING TABLE (fitted with three drawers), on claw and ball feet. From Erthig, Denbighshire. *c.* 1740.

Height, 2 ft 8 ins
Width, 2 ft 10 ins

194. DRESSING TABLE, inlaid with satinwood lines and ebonised wood. *c.* 1775. From the Victoria and Albert Museum.

Height, 2 ft 9 ins
Width, 3 ft 8½ ins

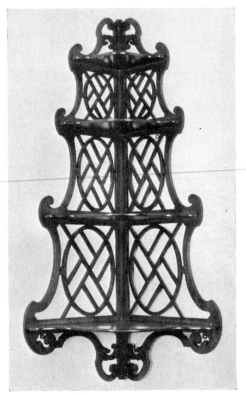

195. HANGING SHELVES, with drawers at base, and veneered with satinwood and cross-banded. *c.* 1780. From the Edward Hudson Collection.

Height, 2 ft $3\frac{1}{2}$ ins
Length, 3 ft $5\frac{3}{4}$ ins

196. ANGLE BRACKET, with four tiers of graduated shelves. Mid-eighteenth century. From Mr. Leonard Knight.

197. DUMB WAITER, with a brass superstructure. From Inveraray Castle, Argyllshire.

Height, 3 ft 5½ ins

198. DRUM-TOPPED TABLE, surmounted by graduated bookshelves. From Messrs. M. Harris.

Fire screens

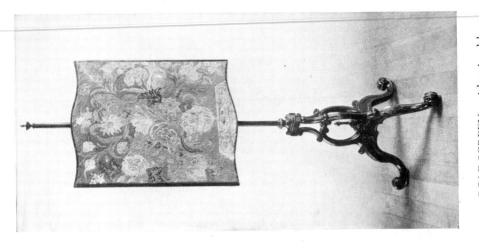

201. POLE SCREEN, with tripod base. From Brigadier W. Clark. *Height*, 5 ft $\frac{3}{4}$ in

200. CHEVAL SCREEN, with carved and pierced cresting. *c.* 1780. From the Frederick Behrens Collection. *Height*, 3 ft 4$\frac{1}{2}$ ins *Width*, 1 ft 10 ins

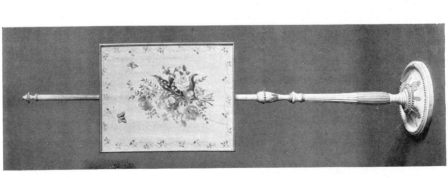

199. POLE SCREEN, of white painted wood with gilt details. *c.* 1775. From Blickling Hall, Norfolk. *Height*, 5 ft 4 ins

INDEX

INDEX